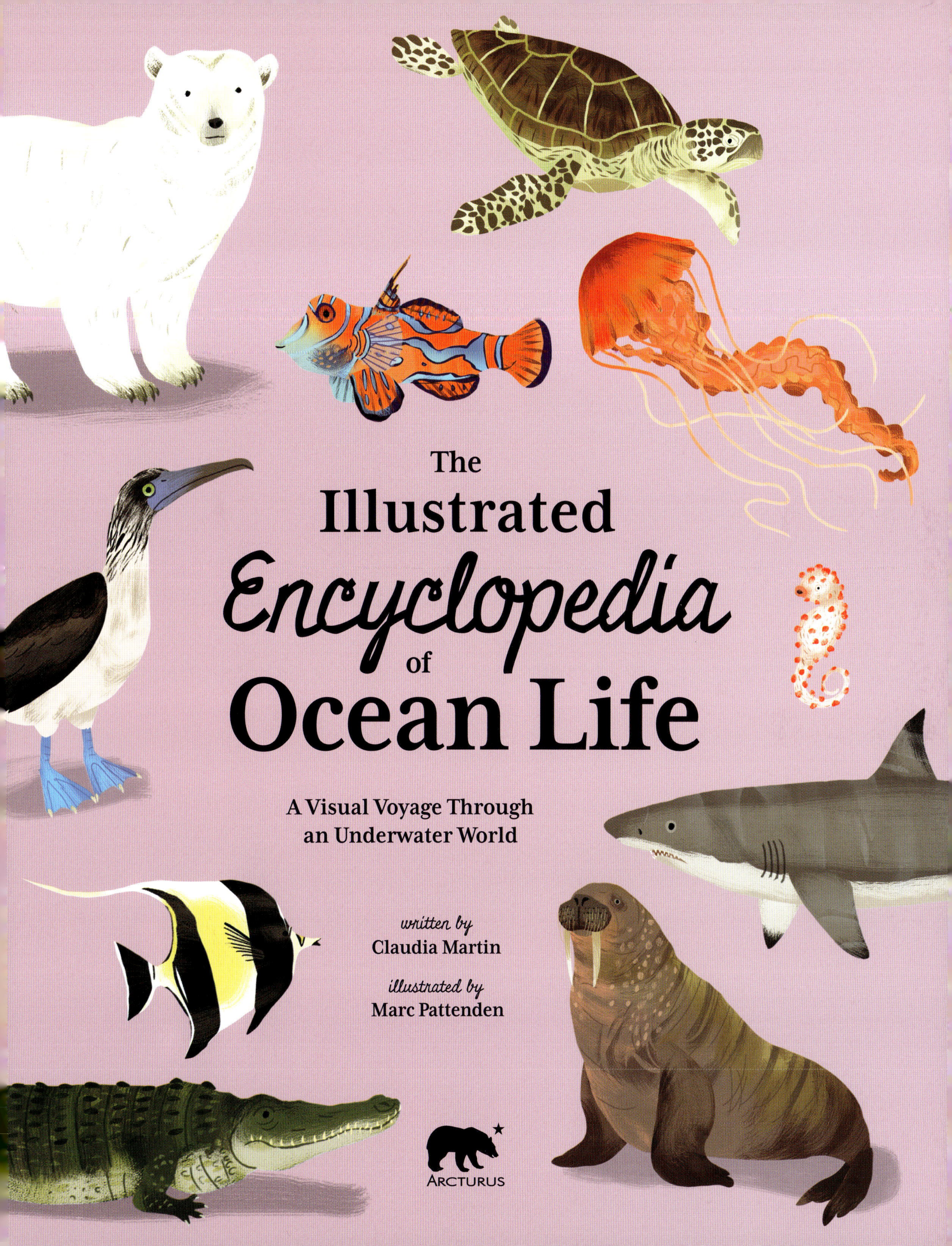

The Illustrated *Encyclopedia* of Ocean Life

A Visual Voyage Through an Underwater World

written by
Claudia Martin

illustrated by
Marc Pattenden

ARCTURUS

ARCTURUS
This edition published in 2025 by Arcturus Publishing Limited
26/27 Bickels Yard, 151–153 Bermondsey Street,
London SE1 3HA

Author: Claudia Martin
Illustrator: Marc Pattenden
Designer: Amy McSimpson
Consultant: Dr. Ross Piper
Editor: Becca Clunes
Design Manager: Rosie Bellwood-Moyler
Editorial Manager: Joe Harris

ISBN: 978-1-3988-5724-7
CH011593US
Supplier 29, Date 0525, PI 00010768

Printed in China

Contents

World of Water

More than 70 percent of Earth's surface is covered by ocean. Dropping to a depth of 10.9 km (6.8 miles), the ocean provides 90 percent of the living space on our planet. It is home to more than 240,000 species of living things that have, so far, been named by scientists. The majority of named species are animals, ranging in size from the blue whale—29.9 m (98 ft) long—to tiny creatures such as jellyfish just 1 cm (0.4 in) across. Ocean animals find shelter and food among many other types of living things. These include plants, seaweeds, and microorganisms too small to be seen by the human eye.

Unlike the world's rivers and lakes, the oceans contain salt water. Around 3.5 percent of salt water is "table salt" (known to scientists as sodium chloride) and other minerals. Over millions of years, these minerals were worn away from Earth's rocks by rain and wind, then carried into the ocean by rivers. All animals need water, which is used for carrying food and other materials around the body. However, many ocean animals—including fish, mammals, reptiles, and birds—cannot survive having too much salt in their body, so they get rid of it in their pee or through body parts called salt glands.

Although our planet is 4.5 billion years old, the oceans did not fill dips in Earth's surface until around 4 billion years ago, when our planet had cooled enough for rain to fall. The oceans were home to the first tiny, simple living things. These microorganisms appeared around 3.8 billion years ago. For a long time, microorganisms were the only living things. It was not until 700 million years ago that the first animals evolved in the oceans. Today, animals can be found in all the ocean's habitats, from the deep, dark seafloor to the coral reefs of sunlit coastal water.

Like most seabirds, the harlequin duck has salt glands in its head, which filter salt out of the duck's blood. The salt leaves the body through the bird's nostrils.

On a coral reef off the coast of Indonesia, fish such as ribbon eels can be spotted. These predators dart from a crevice to catch passing shrimp, such as the harlequin (bottom left). Attached to a rock is an invertebrate (backboneless) animal called an ink-spot sea squirt (middle left), which feeds by sucking in water through its upper tube. Microorganisms are filtered from the water, which is expelled from the squirt's side tube.

Ocean Dwellers

The oceans are home to at least 240,000 types of living things, known as species. Scientists think that many ocean species are yet to be discovered, so there may be a million or more in total. These living things include animals, plants, protists, and fungi.

SCIENTIFIC GROUPS

Scientists have divided living things into groups—such as species, order, class, and kingdom—based on their similarities. A species is a group of living things that look similar and can reproduce together. For example, the hawksbill sea turtle species is in the turtle order, in the reptile class, in the animal kingdom.

KINGDOMS OF LIFE

All living things are made of tiny working parts called cells. They all need food, which they use to make energy, and—at some point in their life—they all grow and move. Living things are often placed in six kingdoms:

BACTERIA:
These tiny living things are made of one simple cell. Some marine bacteria, called cyanobacteria, make their own food from sunlight, while others make it from minerals.

ARCHAEA:
Similar to bacteria, these tiny, single-celled, simple living things may be the most common group in the oceans. Many can live in extreme environments such as super-hot hydrothermal vents.

PLANTS:
Usually green or with green parts, plants are made of many cells. They make their own food from sunlight, so can survive only in water no deeper than 200 m (655 ft).

PROTISTS:
Protists can be made of one cell or many. Some get food by making it from sunlight, like a plant, while others soak it up, like a fungus, or eat other living things, like an animal. Algae such as kelps and other seaweeds are plantlike protists.

FUNGI:
Either many-celled or single-celled, fungi soak up food from their surroundings. Many marine fungi are microscopic, while others are parasites that live on other living things.

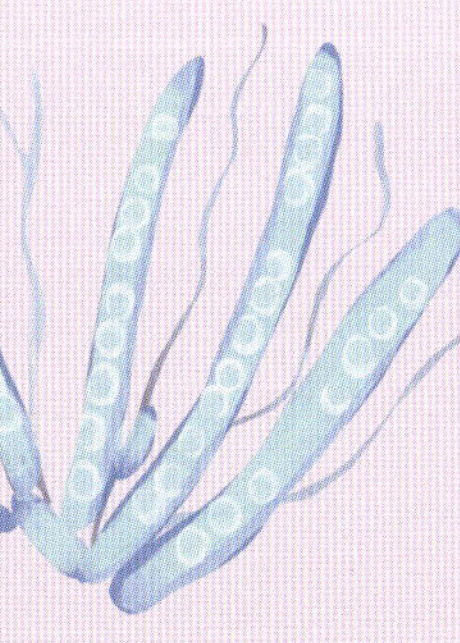

ANIMALS:
Animals are made of many, complex cells. They feed on other living things and need to take in water to transport food around the body. All animals also need to take oxygen from air or water. Oxygen is used as fuel for turning food into energy.

ANIMALS

Animals can be divided into six groups, but only five of them live in the ocean:

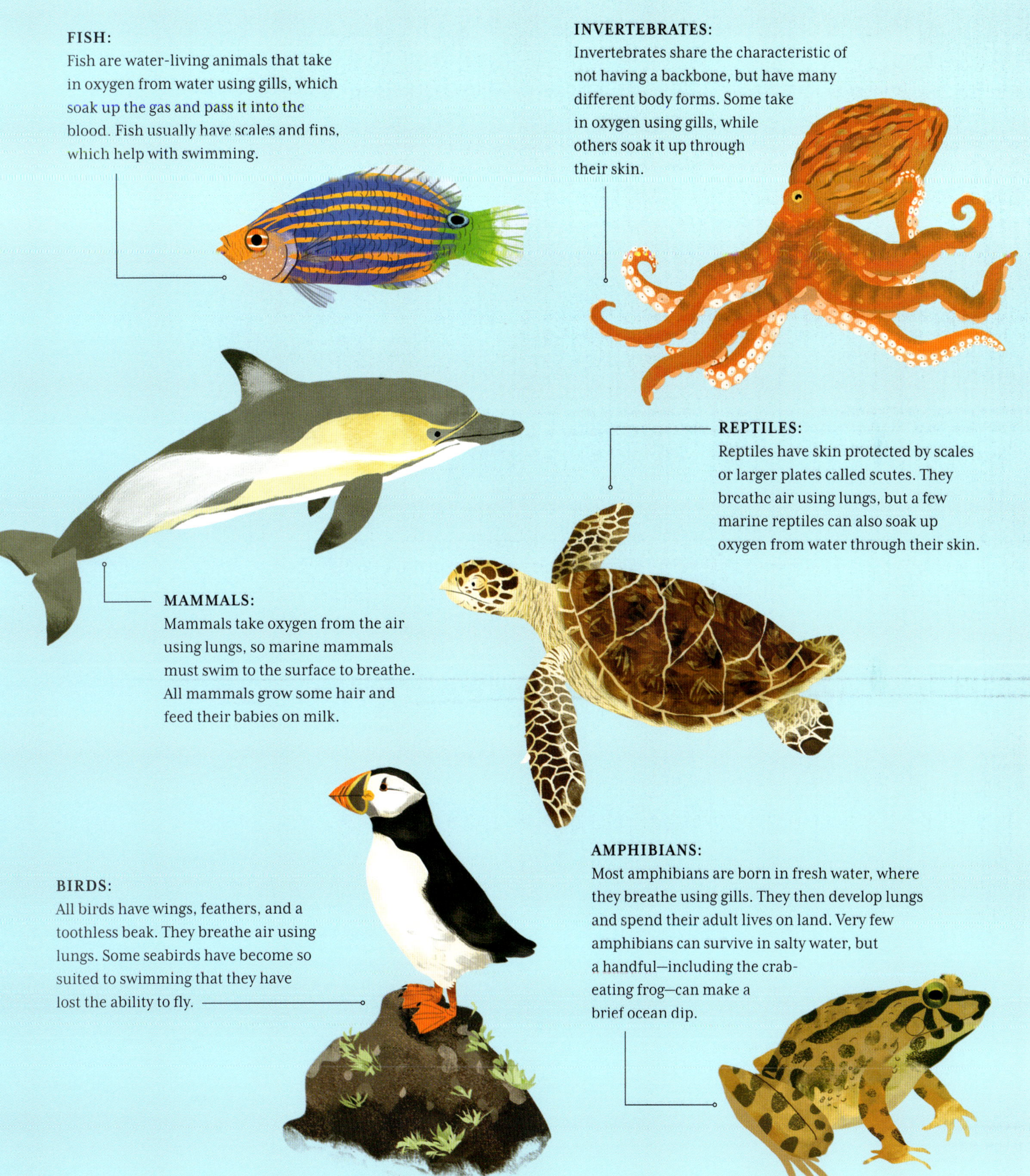

FISH:
Fish are water-living animals that take in oxygen from water using gills, which soak up the gas and pass it into the blood. Fish usually have scales and fins, which help with swimming.

INVERTEBRATES:
Invertebrates share the characteristic of not having a backbone, but have many different body forms. Some take in oxygen using gills, while others soak it up through their skin.

REPTILES:
Reptiles have skin protected by scales or larger plates called scutes. They breathe air using lungs, but a few marine reptiles can also soak up oxygen from water through their skin.

MAMMALS:
Mammals take oxygen from the air using lungs, so marine mammals must swim to the surface to breathe. All mammals grow some hair and feed their babies on milk.

AMPHIBIANS:
Most amphibians are born in fresh water, where they breathe using gills. They then develop lungs and spend their adult lives on land. Very few amphibians can survive in salty water, but a handful—including the crab-eating frog—can make a brief ocean dip.

BIRDS:
All birds have wings, feathers, and a toothless beak. They breathe air using lungs. Some seabirds have become so suited to swimming that they have lost the ability to fly.

Habitats

A habitat is the natural home of a living thing, where it is suited to the conditions. There are many different ocean habitats, due to different conditions such as temperature and depth. Habitats range from the coral reefs of warm, shallow water to the icy chill of the polar ocean.

FIVE OCEANS

Geographers divide the world ocean into five oceans. From largest to smallest, they are the Pacific, Atlantic, Indian, Southern, and Arctic Oceans. The Pacific Ocean covers 168.7 million sq km (65.1 million sq miles), which is more than 44 times the area of the United States. The Pacific is also the deepest ocean, reaching 10,920 m (35,825 ft). The Arctic is the smallest and shallowest ocean, covering 15.6 million sq km (6 million sq miles) and dropping to 5,550 m (18,210 ft).

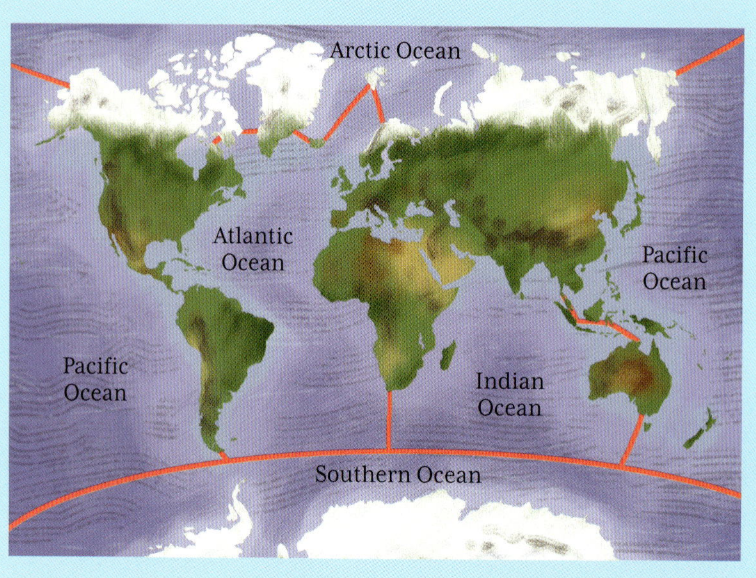

The Red Sea anthias is found only in the Red Sea, a shallow inlet of the Indian Ocean that is one of Earth's warmest areas of seawater. The fish cannot survive temperatures lower than 19 °C (66 °F). Its bright pattern helps it blend in among coral reefs.

TEMPERATURE

The five oceans have different temperature ranges because of their distance from the equator and their currents. Currents are rivers of moving water, caused by wind or by warm water rising and cold water sinking, as can be seen in a pan of heating water. The warmest ocean is the Indian, with a temperature at its surface between 19 and 30 °C (66 and 86 °F). It lies mostly in the tropical zone, which is in a broad band around the equator. To the north and south of this zone is the cooler temperate zone, which covers the northern and southern regions of the Pacific and Atlantic Oceans. The coldest ocean is the Arctic, with a surface temperature of around -2 °C (28 °F). It lies entirely in the polar zone.

This icefish lives only in the Southern Ocean, around Antarctica. Its blood contains an "antifreeze" chemical that stops it from freezing, allowing the fish to survive in water below 0 °C (32 °F). Its translucent (see-through) body helps with camouflage in its icy habitat.

DEPTH ZONES

Different habitats are found at different depths in the oceans, because of the amount of light and warmth that is received from the Sun. Scientists often divide the ocean into three depth zones: sunlight, twilight, and midnight.

Alligator pipefish

SUNLIGHT ZONE: Also known as the epipelagic zone, this region receives enough sunlight and warmth for plants and algae to make their own food. These living things provide food and shelter for others, so this zone is home to 90 percent of all ocean animals. In coastal waters, seagrass meadows, kelp forests, and coral reefs are found.

Portuguese man o' war

Orca

Sunlight zone

200 m (655 ft)

Twilight zone

Sperm whale

Hatchetfish

1,000 m (3,280 ft)

Midnight zone

Deep-sea spider

Anglerfish

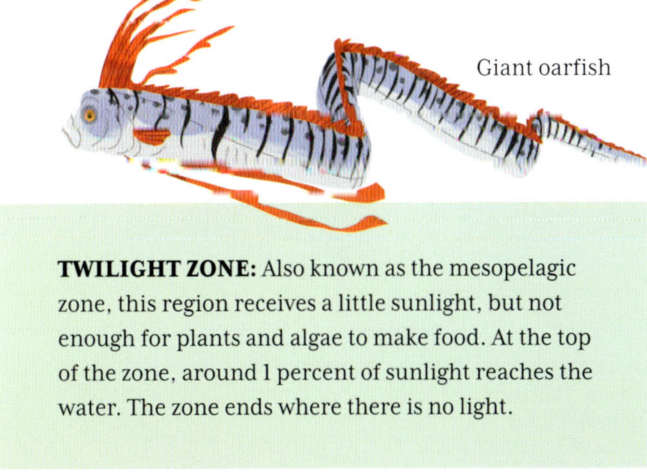

Giant oarfish

TWILIGHT ZONE: Also known as the mesopelagic zone, this region receives a little sunlight, but not enough for plants and algae to make food. At the top of the zone, around 1 percent of sunlight reaches the water. The zone ends where there is no light.

MIDNIGHT ZONE: Also known as the bathypelagic zone, this region is always dark and cool, staying between 2 and 4 °C (36 and 39 °F) in all the world's oceans. Animals here have bodies suited to the harsh conditions and to finding the sparse food.

Spinyhead seadevil

Life Cycles

Most ocean animals lay eggs, while others give birth to live young. A few invertebrates divide themselves into two to make a new animal. Some animals are born as smaller versions of their adult selves, while others change their body form as they grow, in a process called metamorphosis.

LAYING EGGS

All birds and most invertebrates, fish, amphibians, and reptiles lay eggs. The majority of female fish release a large number of undeveloped eggs into water, where they are fertilized by a male fish's sperm. These eggs are jelly-like and would dry out in air. Birds and egg-laying reptiles lay a smaller number of shelled eggs on land.

A female sockeye salmon releases her eggs into a river. The young fish spend one or two years in fresh water before migrating to the Pacific Ocean as adults.

Like most reptiles, the loggerhead sea turtle hatches from a rubbery-shelled egg that was laid on land.

LIVE BIRTH

All marine mammals and a few fish, reptiles, and invertebrates give birth to live young. Live birth can happen in two ways: ovoviviparity and viviparity. Most sea snakes and some fish, such as great white sharks, are ovoviviparous: The mother carries fertilized eggs inside her until they hatch, with each egg containing its own supply of food.

Marine mammals and some fish, such as hammerhead sharks, are viviparous: The mother carries her developing baby or babies inside her, supplying them with food from her own blood.

The common minke whale is a mammal. It is viviparous: It gives birth to one calf every two or three years. Viviparous mothers produce fewer babies than mothers that lay eggs or are ovoviviparous, due to the effort of feeding the baby inside them. However, they usually give their young a good chance of survival by caring for them until they can survive alone.

METAMORPHOSIS

Many invertebrates, fish, and amphibians go through metamorphosis. The name for a young animal that has not yet gone through metamorphosis is "larva." During metamorphosis, an animal goes through changes to its body, diet, and lifestyle. One advantage of metamorphosis is that larvae eat different food from adults, which prevents competition between them. In addition, many animals that stay fixed to one spot as adults—such as corals and sponges—spend time as a floating or swimming larva, which allows them to find a suitable spot to settle, away from their parent.

Most cartilage-skeletoned fish, such as sharks, do not metamorphose, but most other fish do. They hatch from their egg as a non-swimming larva, still attached to a bag of food called a yolk sac. Over days or weeks, a young fish loses its yolk sac, grows fins, and takes its adult form.

A red rock crab is an invertebrate that lives on rocky seashores. A female carries her fertilized eggs beneath her tail. When the eggs hatch, she releases them into the ocean.

After a larva metamorphoses into a young adult, it swims ashore. As it grows, it sheds its shell whenever it becomes too small, revealing a brighter shell beneath.

A larva drifts in the ocean, protected by its sharp spines.

Oceans at Risk

More than 2,000 marine animals are at risk of becoming extinct. Many endangered animals live in the coastal ocean or nest on coasts, which are at higher risk from threats such as pollution and habitat loss. Other threatened species are particularly sensitive to rising temperatures.

GLOBAL WARMING

The temperatures of Earth's oceans and air have risen by around 1 °C (1.8 °F) since 1900. Much of the rise has been caused by the burning of fuels such as coal, oil, and natural gas. This releases carbon dioxide gas, which traps the Sun's heat in the atmosphere. The temperature rise is shrinking the ice that covers the Arctic Ocean, damaging the habitat of polar bears and walruses. Warming oceans are also damaging coral reefs. Many corals take much of their food from algae that live inside them, where the algae make food from sunlight. When the water warms, stressed corals expel their algae, leaving themselves at risk of starvation.

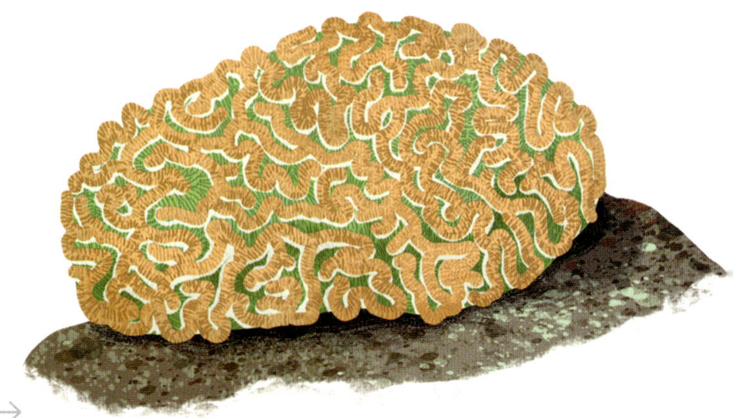

HABITAT LOSS

Habitats from mangrove forests to coral reefs are being damaged by construction along coasts, seabed mining, and careless fishing methods. The dugong is being threatened by the loss of its coastal seagrass habitat.

POLLUTION

Pollution of ocean water by human waste, oil spills, and farming and factory chemicals can put animals at risk. The red handfish is found only on the coast of Australia's Tasmania, where it is threatened by pollution from nearby towns and farms.

OVERFISHING

Overfishing is when too many animals in a species are caught, leaving the remaining animals unable to produce enough babies to keep up their numbers. Sharks are particularly at risk from overfishing because they are caught for food and for their cartilage and liver oil, which are used in cosmetics. Around a third of shark species, including the sand tiger, are threatened.

INVASIVE SPECIES

Invasive species are animals that are not found naturally in a habitat but are taken there, by accident or on purpose, by humans. Seabirds may be killed or have their eggs eaten by species introduced to the islands where they nest. The Galápagos penguin, which lives farther north than other penguins, on the equatorial Galápagos Islands, is at risk from invasive rats and cats.

PET TRADE

Some marine animals, such as the Banggai cardinalfish, are captured in large numbers so they can be sold as pets. Today, laws aim to protect these animals by forbidding the sale of endangered animals that have been captured from the wild, rather than born in aquariums.

Invertebrates

Invertebrates make up more than 90 percent of ocean-living animal species. Invertebrates (meaning "without a backbone" in Latin) share a basic characteristic: They do not have a spine. Apart from this feature, invertebrates have countless differences, with many body shapes and lifestyles. Based on their different body forms, scientists divide invertebrates into large groups called phyla (singular: phylum; plural: phyla). There are more than 30 phyla. Among the largest are arthropods, mollusks, cnidarians, echinoderms, annelids, and poriferans.

Arthropods have a body divided into parts called segments. The body is protected by a tough outer covering called an exoskeleton. Their legs have bendable joints. Ocean arthropods include many well-known animals, such as crustaceans—lobsters, crabs, and shrimp—and sea spiders. Another huge phylum is the mollusks. These animals have a muscly body. Some, such as sea snails and mussels, live inside a shell. Others—including sea slugs, octopuses, and squid—do not.

Cnidarians—such as jellyfish, corals, and sea anemones—have stingers. Echinoderms include starfish (also called sea stars), sea cucumbers, and sea urchins. These animals usually live on the seafloor and have tough skin. Other common phyla include the annelids, which are worms with a segmented body; and poriferans, often called sponges, which have a body full of holes and channels.

Named after a sailing ship, the Portuguese man o' war belongs to the cnidarian phylum. Its gas-filled bag floats at the ocean surface, while its trailing tentacles give deadly stings to prey such as fish. The man o' war is not a single animal: It is made up of many similar animals, which dangle from the shared bag.

Lobsters and Relatives

Like crabs and shrimp, lobsters are crustaceans. This means they have a body with many segments, covered by a shell-like exoskeleton. Lobsters have ten walking legs for crawling on the seafloor, but up to 38 wiggly, leglike appendages in total, including antennae for sensing.

EUROPEAN LOBSTER

Like other true lobsters, this lobster has pincer-like claws on its front three pairs of legs. The front claws are largest, with the front left claw usually biggest of all. Called the "crusher," this knobbly claw is for crushing prey. The front right claw, the "cutter," has sharp edges for tearing prey.

RED REEF LOBSTER

This small reef lobster spends its days in holes on the coral reefs of the Indian and Pacific Oceans. At night, it crawls out in search of shrimp, crabs, and worms. Unlike true lobsters, reef lobsters have claws only on their first pair of walking legs.

CARIBBEAN SPINY LOBSTER

Unlike true lobsters, spiny lobsters are usually clawless and have longer, thicker, spinier antennae. The Caribbean spiny lobster uses its antennae during migrations to avoid winter storms: Groups of lobsters walk across the seafloor, using their antennae to feel the route and each other.

TERRIBLE CLAW LOBSTER

Most lobsters live in shallow water not far from land. Yet this true lobster, which is blind, lives on dark seafloors as deep as 250 m (820 ft). One of its front claws is much longer than the other and armed with long prickles. This claw may be used for fighting other lobsters.

MUSICAL FURRY LOBSTER

The musical furry lobster is named for making a loud rasping noise to scare away predators. The noise is produced by rubbing bumps on its antenna against plates below its eyes. Like most crustaceans, this spiny lobster must shed its hard shell regularly as it grows.

JAPANESE MITTEN LOBSTER

Part of the slipper lobster family, this clawless lobster has wide, flat antennae that make it look like a mitten. These antennae are used for digging in the sandy seafloor so the lobster can hide. Unlike many lobsters, which have eyes on stalks, this lobster's eyes are in sockets inside its head.

Lobster Facts

ORDER	Decapods ("ten-footed")
PHYLUM	Arthropods
SIZE	4–64 cm (1.6–25 in) long
RANGE	Seafloor of all oceans
DIET	Fish, invertebrates, plants, and dead, rotting animals

Peacock Mantis Shrimp

The 520 species of mantis shrimp take their name from the insects called mantises. Like those insects, these shrimp use their strong front legs for killing prey. This mantis shrimp has an eye-catchingly patterned shell, which—like the feathers of a peacock—helps the shrimp to attract a mate.

SHELLED BODY

The peacock mantis shrimp is a crustacean, which means it has a segmented body covered by a shell. Its segments are grouped into two main body parts: a cephalothorax (a head fused with a thorax, holding the brain, heart, and stomach) and a muscly abdomen, which ends in a tail.

LOTS OF LEGS

At the front of the shrimp's cephalothorax are two pairs of antennae for touching, tasting, and smelling. The shrimp also has a pair of eyes on stalks, which can turn in different directions from each other. Near the eyes are large, green, shiny, teardrop-shaped scales, called antennal scales. The brightness of these scales helps to attract a mate.

The next appendages on the cephalothorax are five pairs of maxillipeds ("mouthpart legs"). The first pair, used for cleaning, are small and close to the mouth. The next pair are used for punching prey: They are large, shaped like clubs, and covered by extra-thick shell. The other maxillipeds, which end in a flat plate, are for passing food to the mouth.

The peacock mantis shrimp has compound eyes, which have tens of thousands of lenses, each pointing in a slightly different direction. This helps the shrimp to see fast movement all around. Mantis shrimp can also see types of light that humans cannot, including ultraviolet, which helps them see light flashing from the antennal scales of other shrimp.

The peacock mantis shrimp also has another 18 appendages to help with movement, both on the seafloor and when swimming. The cephalothorax has three pairs of pereiopods ("walking legs"); the abdomen has five pairs of pleopods ("swimming legs") and a pair of uropods ("tail legs") to help with steering through the water.

PACKING A PUNCH

This mantis shrimp spends much of its time hiding in a U-shaped hole that it burrows in the sand around coral reefs. When it is hungry, it sets out to hunt, usually for small, shelled invertebrates. When the mantis shrimp gets close to prey, it uses its clublike maxillipeds to punch again and again until the prey's shell breaks. Then it feeds on the soft body inside.

The peacock mantis shrimp has the fastest known punch of any animal, up to 80 km/h (50 miles per hour). As well as cracking the shell, the force of each punch makes bubbles of gas inside the prey's body. When these bubbles pop, they release heat, damaging the unlucky prey's shell yet more.

Peacock Mantis Shrimp Facts

SPECIES	*Odontodactylus scyllarus*
ORDER	Mantis shrimp
PHYLUM	Arthropods
SIZE	5–18 cm (2–7 in) long
RANGE	Coral reefs of the Indian and western Pacific Oceans
DIET	Snails, crabs, shrimp, and scallops

On the Sand

Invertebrates scuttle, burrow, and hunt on a sandy beach in Malaysia, in Southeast Asia. As the ocean rises up the shore at high tide, then draws out again at low tide, these animals must adapt to the constantly changing conditions.

The intertidal zone—the area of beach that is under water at high tide but exposed to the air at low tide—is a challenging habitat. Many intertidal invertebrates are burrowers. A burrow protects them from predators; from drying out in sunshine and wind at low tide; and from being washed away at high tide.

Invertebrates here include crustaceans such as true crabs and mole crabs, both with shells and ten legs. There are also bivalve mollusks, including clams, their legless, soft bodies protected by a hinged, two-part shell. Six-legged insects, such as tiger beetles, run to high ground when the water rises.

PERPLEXING FIDDLER CRAB

Like other true crabs, the perplexing fiddler has eyes on movable stalks—giving it a wider, higher view of the beach—and claws on its front pair of legs, which it uses for catching prey. Males have one much larger claw, which they wave to attract a female. The higher a male waves, the better his chance of success.

HIPPA MOLE CRAB

Unlike a true crab, a mole crab cannot walk on its ten legs. It uses its legs to dig a burrow, which it does backward, keeping its mouth toward the surface. The mole crab's long, rounded body is suited to fast burrowing. When the tide rises, the mole crab seizes tiny floating creatures with its antennae.

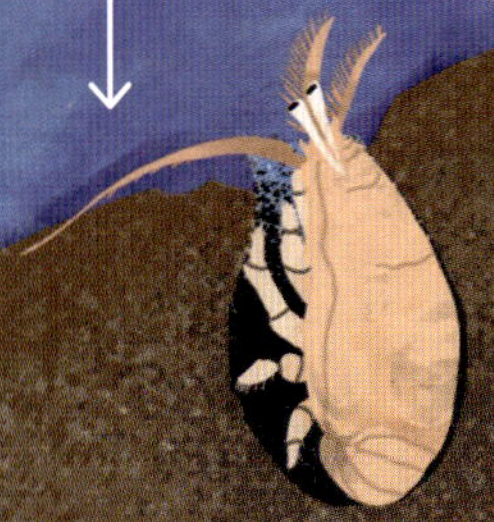

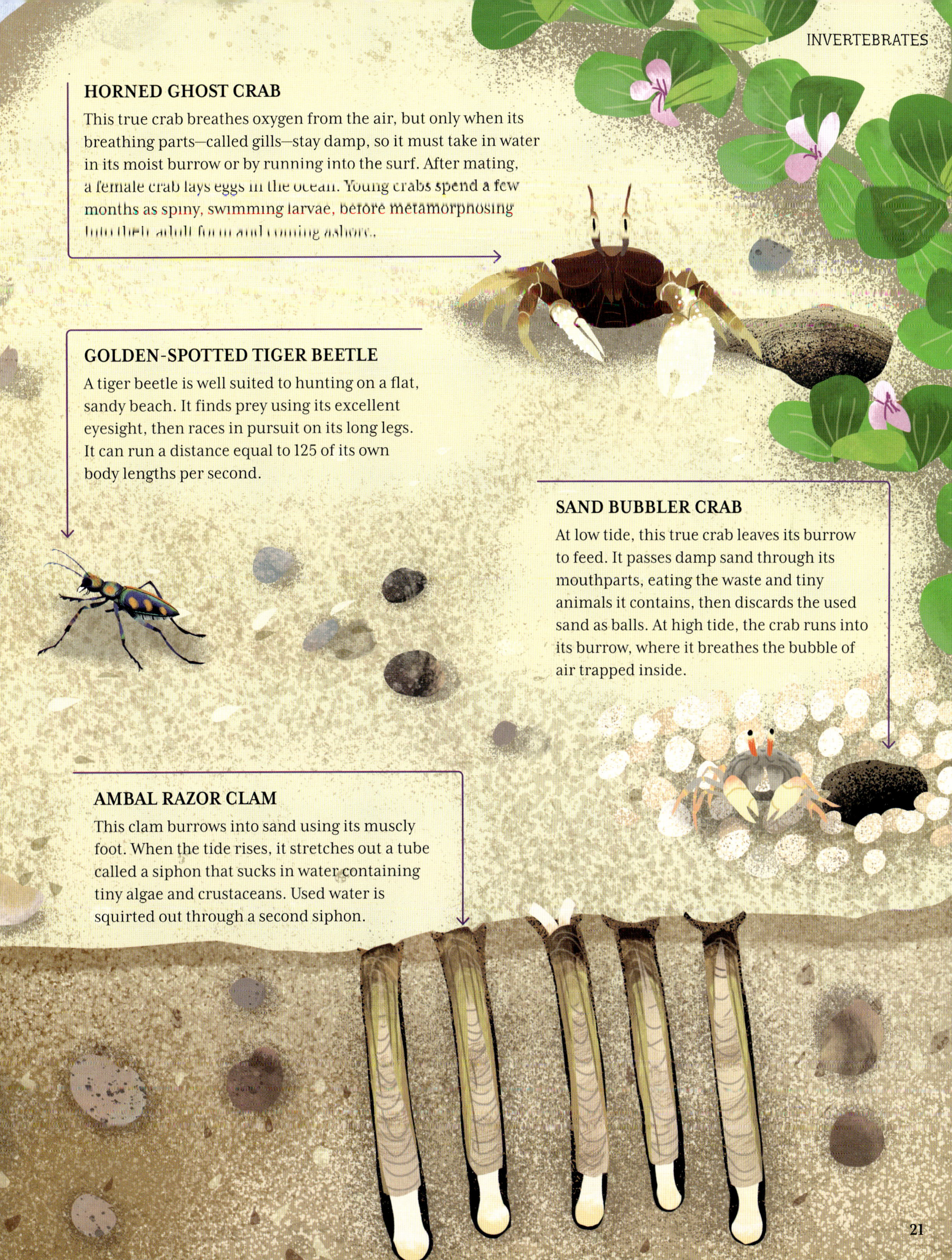

HORNED GHOST CRAB

This true crab breathes oxygen from the air, but only when its breathing parts—called gills—stay damp, so it must take in water in its moist burrow or by running into the surf. After mating, a female crab lays eggs in the ocean. Young crabs spend a few months as spiny, swimming larvae, before metamorphosing into their adult form and coming ashore.

GOLDEN-SPOTTED TIGER BEETLE

A tiger beetle is well suited to hunting on a flat, sandy beach. It finds prey using its excellent eyesight, then races in pursuit on its long legs. It can run a distance equal to 125 of its own body lengths per second.

SAND BUBBLER CRAB

At low tide, this true crab leaves its burrow to feed. It passes damp sand through its mouthparts, eating the waste and tiny animals it contains, then discards the used sand as balls. At high tide, the crab runs into its burrow, where it breathes the bubble of air trapped inside.

AMBAL RAZOR CLAM

This clam burrows into sand using its muscly foot. When the tide rises, it stretches out a tube called a siphon that sucks in water containing tiny algae and crustaceans. Used water is squirted out through a second siphon.

Anemone Hermit Crab

Unlike true crabs, hermit crabs do not have a shell of their own. To protect their soft body, they live in the abandoned shell of a sea snail. The anemone hermit crab also has an extra way to protect itself from predators: It decorates its borrowed shell with stinging sea anemones.

FINDING SHELLS

The anemone hermit crab is one of more than 800 species of hermit crabs. Although it is a ten-legged crustacean like a crab or lobster, its exoskeleton—outer covering—is not hard, because it does not contain lots of the hard mineral calcium carbonate. The hermit crab's abdomen is soft and curves in a spiral, like the inside of the snail shells that it occupies.

As a hermit crab grows larger, it must find a new, bigger shell regularly. It looks for snail shells on the ocean floor, either abandoned by a bigger hermit crab or left empty after the snail has been eaten by a predator. The chosen shell must be large enough for the hermit crab to pull its whole body inside if attacked. When not hiding, a hermit crab's cephalothorax and front three pairs of legs stick out from the shell so that it can walk across the seafloor. The back two pairs of legs hold the hermit crab inside its shell.

Hermit crabs have been known to form lines for shell swapping, with larger shells swapped down the line, from bigger to smaller hermit crabs. However, if there is a shortage of suitable homes, a hermit crab may steal from another hermit crab by loudly hitting the victim's shell with its own shell until the victim gives in.

ATTACHING ANEMONES

This hermit crab collects sea anemones using its front legs, particularly the first pair, which end in claws. The hermit crab taps and strokes an anemone until it lets go of the rock or coral on which it is living. Related to jellyfish and corals, sea anemones are invertebrates with many stinging tentacles. The hermit crab then plants the sea anemone on its shell.

Wearing anemones helps to protect this hermit crab from its main predators, which are octopuses. The anemones also benefit from this relationship, since they use their tentacles to catch scraps of food that float away as the hermit crab eats its meals messily.

Anemone Hermit Crab Facts

SPECIES	*Dardanus pedunculatus*
ORDER	Decapods ("ten-footed")
PHYLUM	Arthropods
SIZE	8–10 cm (3–4 in) long
RANGE	Coral reefs of the Indian and western Pacific Oceans
DIET	Fish, snails, worms, and algae

When changing shells, an anemone hermit crab also moves its anemones onto the new shell.

Coral

Most corals live in groups, called colonies, which are attached to the seafloor. A colony is home to many identical coral animals, known as polyps. Each polyp has a mouth surrounded by stinging tentacles for catching food. For protection, some coral polyps—known as stony corals—make rocklike exoskeletons, which can form huge coral reefs.

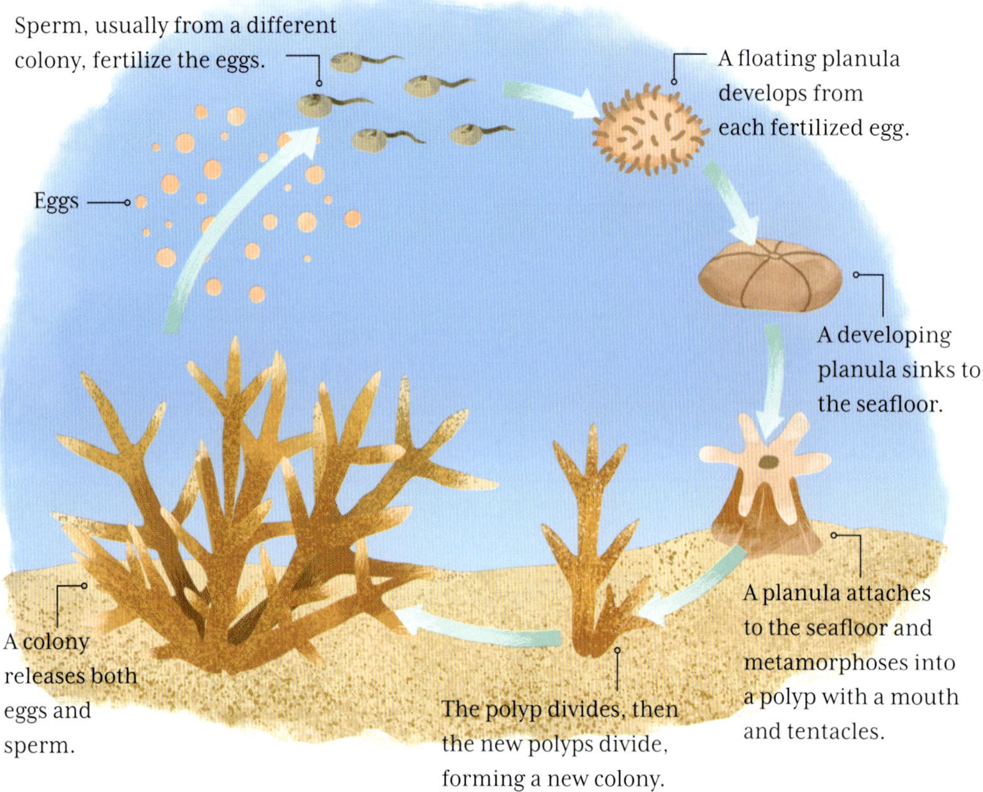

STAGHORN CORAL

A staghorn coral colony has rocklike branches formed by the exoskeletons of thousands of tiny polyps. Colonies can reproduce in two ways. The first is when branches break from the colony and attach to the seafloor, then the polyps divide to create new polyps. The second is when, once a year, colonies release eggs and sperm, as shown on the left.

BOULDER BRAIN CORAL

This stony coral makes a domed colony that resembles a wrinkled human brain. At night, the colony's many polyps stretch out their tentacles to catch tiny floating animals. The polyps also take food from algae that live inside their body. The algae make their own food from sunlight, so this coral is found only in shallow, sunlit water.

ORANGE CUP CORAL

Unlike many corals, this stony coral does not house sunlight-needing algae, so it can live in deeper, darker waters. It lives in small colonies of no more than a hundred polyps. Each polyp is brainless, but can smell and taste passing prey.

FUNGIA MUSHROOM CORAL

This unusual stony coral is solitary, which means each polyp lives alone. A polyp has a central mouth surrounded by a round stony disk up to 30 cm (12 in) wide. While most coral polyps remain in one spot, this one detaches from the seafloor then crawls, by stretching and squeezing, to a new spot.

PURPLE SEA FAN

Up to 1.5 m (4.9 ft) tall, the purple sea fan is a soft coral, which means that its polyps do not build rocklike exoskeletons. Thousands of polyps live along each colony's branching stems, which are made of a bendy material called gorgonin. The fan grows at right angles to the water current, which carries floating food to all the polyps.

CARNATION CORAL

Carnation coral polyps are soft corals. Although these corals do not help to make reefs, they often attach to them. Colonies form branching, treelike shapes.

Coral Facts

CLASS	Anthozoans
PHYLUM	Cnidarians
SIZE	Up to 22 m (72 ft) wide for a colony
RANGE	Seafloor of all oceans
DIET	Specks of waste, small fish, zooplankton (drifting tiny animals), and sugar made by in-body algae

Black Sea Nettle

This jellyfish is called a sea nettle due to its painful stings, which feel like the stings of the land plants known as nettles. The black sea nettle swims by expanding then squeezing its soft, umbrella-shaped body. This action shoots water behind the jellyfish—which pushes the jellyfish forward.

Black Sea Nettle Facts

SPECIES	*Chrysaora achlyos*
CLASS	True jellyfish
PHYLUM	Cnidarians
SIZE	6–7.6 m (20–25 ft) long
RANGE	Eastern Pacific Ocean
DIET	Zooplankton and small jellyfish

BRAINLESS BODY

The black sea nettle's body, called a bell, grows up to 1 m (3.3 ft) wide. In the middle of the bell's underside is a mouth, which opens directly to the jellyfish's stomach. After eating, poop is also released from the mouth. The jellyfish has no brain, but it does have a network of nerves and sense organs that allow it to detect light and direction, and to smell and taste the chemicals given off by prey and predators. The jellyfish has no lungs or gills, but it soaks up oxygen from the water through its skin.

STINGING TENTACLES

From the edge of this jellyfish's bell, 24 slim tentacles trail through the water. Each tentacle is covered with thousands of stingers, called nematocysts. When prey or a predator touches a nematocyst, it fires a needle-like spine that is coated in venom. This injects venom into the animal. Small prey is killed immediately. Larger predators and prey may be stunned and unable to move. The black sea nettle's mouth is surrounded by four thicker, ruffled oral arms, which stretch and bend to pass food to the jellyfish's mouth.

A black sea nettle polyp feeds on passing zooplankton using its tentacles.

A budding polyp absorbs its tentacles, then releases 5 to 15 identical segments called ephyrae.

COMPLICATED LIFE

Like other jellyfish—as well as other cnidarians such as corals and sea anemones—the black sea nettle goes through metamorphosis. Adults are known as medusas. Male sea nettle medusas release sperm into the water. Females release eggs that cling to their upper oral arms. As female medusas swim along, their eggs are fertilized by sperm.

Each fertilized egg develops into a planula (see "Stagorn Coral" on page 24), which detaches from the female and settles on the seabed, where it metamorphoses into a stalked, tentacled polyp. After months or even years, the polyp starts to bud: Segments separate and float away. Each segment, known as an ephyra, develops into a medusa.

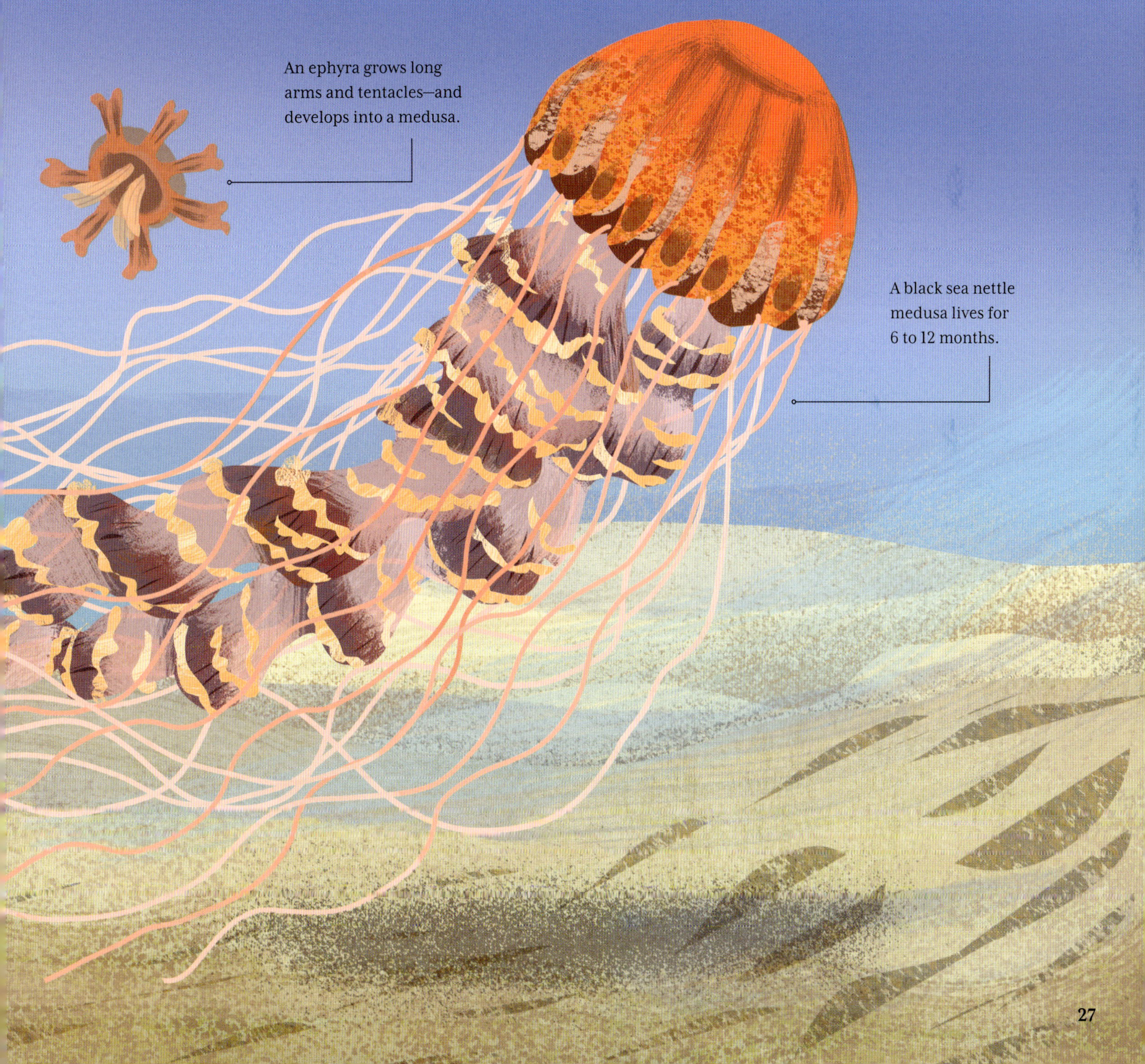

An ephyra grows long arms and tentacles—and develops into a medusa.

A black sea nettle medusa lives for 6 to 12 months.

In a Tide Pool

Puget Sound is an inlet of the Pacific Ocean in the northwest United States. At high tide, rocks in the intertidal zone are covered by seawater. At low tide, when the sea draws out, dips in these rocks are still filled with water, forming tide pools.

Many invertebrates that live in tide pools and on rocky shores are sessile, which means that they do not move around. These animals include bivalve mollusks, such as mussels, and crustaceans, such as barnacles, which stick themselves to rocks so they are not washed away. They close their shells at low tide to keep themselves from drying out.

Non-sessile animals on this shore include chitons and sea stars, which are also known as starfish. Sea stars, which crawl to stay beneath the tide level, have extra-thick skin so they do not dry out quickly if exposed to the air. Chitons can breathe both underwater and in air, as long as their gills stay damp.

PURPLE SEA STAR

Clinging to rocks with the small, sucker-like "tube feet" on the undersides of its five arms, this sea star crawls onto prey, such as a mussel. It opens the mussel's shell using its tube feet. It sticks its stomach out through its mouth, which is in the middle of its underside, soaks the prey in digestive juices to break it down—then pulls inside the stomach and mushy prey.

CALIFORNIA MUSSEL

This mollusk has a two-part shell. It attaches to rocks using sticky threads. When the tide is high, the mussel opens its shell to stick out a siphon, which sucks in seawater containing zooplankton and oxygen. These are filtered from the water by the mussel's sieve-like gills.

HAIRY CHITON

Living on and under rocks in the intertidal zone, this mollusk feeds on algae and small animals. Its eight-part shell—embedded in its muscly back—gives it freedom of movement: It can crawl on uneven surfaces and curl into a ball for protection. The chiton's bristles help with trapping prey.

COMMON ACORN BARNACLE

Acorn barnacles spend their early lives as swimming larvae. As adults, they cement themselves to a rock, then build six hard plates to protect their soft body, as well as "door" plates to close the top of this shell. When the tide rises, they open the "door" and stick out 12 feathery legs to trap zooplankton.

CRUMB-OF-BREAD SPONGE

Sponges are very simple animals. As adults, they are sessile, but sponge larvae swim until they find a suitable spot to settle. Adults have many holes and tubes through which seawater flows. The walls of these tubes soak up oxygen and food specks.

AGGREGATING ANEMONE

This sea anemone stings small crabs and fish with its tentacles, which are in rows around its central mouth. The aggregating anemone can create copies—clones—of itself by splitting in two. If an anemone that is not a clone enters the anemone's tide pool, it stings the intruder until it leaves or dies.

Cluster Duster

This worm belongs to the family of feather duster worms. The family is named for their feathery tentacles, which look like old-fashioned cleaning equipment. The cluster duster lives in groups on the seafloor. Although the worms in this species have many different shades of tentacles, from brown to orange or purple, worms in the same group usually have matching tentacles.

Cluster duster groups live in warm, sunlit waters no more than 35 m (115 ft) deep. They prefer spots with plenty of water movement to carry food to their tentacles.

BUILDING A TUBE

Like other feather duster worms, the cluster duster is a bristle worm: an invertebrate with a long, soft, segmented body. Although many bristle worms crawl around, adult feather duster worms are sessile, which means they stay in one spot. An adult cluster duster lives inside a strong tube that it attaches to a hard surface such as stony coral or rock. Each of its body segments has hooked bristles that help it cling to—and move up and down inside—this tube.

An adult cluster duster makes its tube from sticky mucus mixed with floating sand caught by its tentacles. The mucus is made in body parts called glands, at the base of the worm's head.

Cluster Duster Facts

SPECIES	*Bispira brunnea*
CLASS	Bristle worms
PHYLUM	Annelids
SIZE	6–10 cm (2.4–4 in) long
RANGE	Shallow seafloor of the Caribbean Sea in the western Atlantic Ocean
DIET	Zooplankton and food specks

FEATHERY FOOD-CATCHERS

When feeding, the cluster duster pokes its head out of the top of its tube. The head has a small brain, a mouth, sense organs, and 18 to 28 feathery tentacles called radioles. Tiny floating animals are trapped in these tentacles, then slide down slippery grooves in each tentacle to the worm's mouth. The tentacles also soak up oxygen from the water.

The worm's sense organs are basic, but they respond to light and to water movements. This means the worm can detect a sudden shadow or ripple that suggests a predator is approaching. If the cluster duster senses danger, it pulls its tentacles inside its tube.

MAKING NEW WORMS

If the cluster duster's tentacles are damaged by a predator—such as a fish or crab—it can grow new ones in a few weeks. It can also reproduce by fragmentation, which means that it splits off parts of itself that grow into new worms.

In addition, cluster dusters can reproduce by releasing either eggs or sperm into the water. Once an egg is fertilized by a sperm, it develops into a floating larva, which eventually settles on the seafloor and metamorphoses into its adult form.

Octopuses

There are around 300 species of octopus, which means "eight feet" in ancient Greek. Octopuses have eight limbs, two eyes, a sharp-beaked mouth, a large brain, and a soft body. Along with other cephalopod mollusks—including squid and cuttlefish—they are probably the most intelligent invertebrates.

COMMON OCTOPUS

Like other cephalopods, this octopus swims by sucking water into its bag-shaped body, then squirting it out through a tube. The backward water jet pushes the octopus forward. Like most cephalopods, this octopus can squirt a cloud of black ink if it is attacked. The ink confuses the attacker for long enough for the octopus to escape.

GREATER BLUE-RINGED OCTOPUS

When this octopus feels threatened, rings of bright blue flash on its yellowish skin. If this warning is ignored, the octopus bites with its hard beak, soaking the attacker's wound with venomous spit. The venom kills most predators or prey within minutes.

COCONUT OCTOPUS

Using its sucker-covered limbs, this small octopus collects shells, which it hides inside when it sees a predator. It also tries to confuse predators by walking across the seafloor on two legs while waving the other six, so it looks like a clump of seaweed.

DUMBO OCTOPUS

This unusual, deep-sea octopus has two fins, which it uses for swimming. These fins resemble the ears of the flying elephant in the 1941 movie *Dumbo*. A dumbo spends most of its time crawling across the seafloor, where it traps worms and shrimp with its eight limbs.

MIMIC OCTOPUS

Like most octopuses, the mimic uses color-changing cells in its skin to blend in with its surroundings. However, this octopus also scares away predators by changing color—and positioning its body and limbs—to match the patterns and appearances of venomous animals such as jellyfish, sea snakes, and zebra soles (pictured).

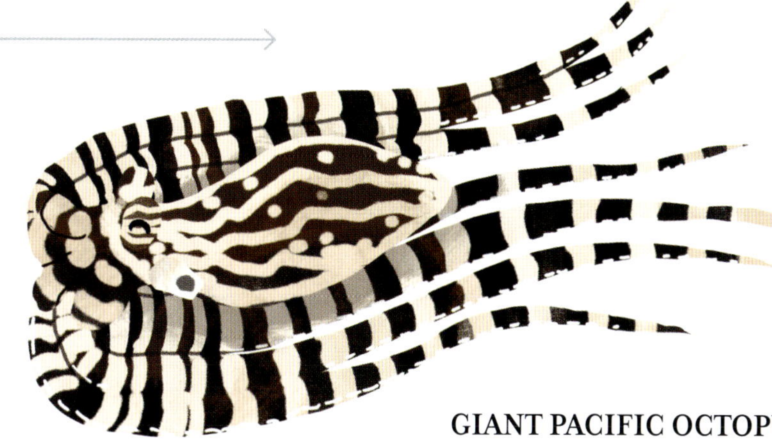

GIANT PACIFIC OCTOPUS

The world's largest octopus, the giant Pacific can weigh up to 50 kg (110 lb). A female mates only once, laying up to 400,000 eggs on a rock. She watches over her eggs so closely, never leaving to find food, that she dies soon after the eggs hatch. Very few hatchlings survive to adulthood.

Octopus Facts

ORDER	Octopuses
CLASS	Cephalopods ("head feet")
PHYLUM	Mollusks
SIZE	2.5 cm–6 m (1 in–19.7 ft) long
RANGE	All oceans
DIET	Fish, crabs, clams, snails, and worms

Giant Squid

Perhaps the largest of all invertebrates, the giant squid reaches 13 m (42.7 ft) long, including its tentacles. It weighs up to 275 kg (600 lb)—more than three times an average adult man. This squid lives in the deep, dark ocean, so it is rarely seen by humans. The first photograph of a live, adult giant squid was not taken until 2002.

Giant Squid Facts

SPECIES	*Architeuthis dux*
CLASS	Cephalopods ("head feet")
PHYLUM	Mollusks
SIZE	10–13 m (33–42.7 ft) long
RANGE	300–1,000 m (980–3,280 ft) deep in all oceans
DIET	Deep-sea fish and squid

CATCHING PREY

Like all squid, the giant squid has eight limbs and two longer tentacles. The tentacles are used to grab prey, while the eight limbs are used to hold it. The inside surfaces of the arms and tentacles are covered by cup-shaped suckers, which stick to prey through suction. The edges of the cups also have sharp teeth, like the blade of a saw, which fix into prey's flesh.

The limbs pass prey to the squid's beak-like mouth, which lies between the limbs, at their base. The beak slices food into bite-size pieces. The squid's tongue, which has small teeth, then shreds food.

Sperm whales (right) are large mammals that often prey on giant squid (left). It is common to see circular scars from giant squid suckers on the heads of sperm whales, which suggests that the squid try to defend themselves. However, a sperm whale is around 100 times heavier than a giant squid, so is likely to win the battle.

SWIMMING ALONG

The giant squid has a soft body called a mantle. It swims by relaxing its mantle muscles, which enlarges the cavity inside, making water flow into the cavity to fill the space. The squid then tightens its muscles to squirt out the water through a tube-like siphon. The squid moves in the opposite direction from where the siphon is pointing: The backward force of the water results in a forward pushing force. The squid can turn the siphon to change direction. In addition, the squid has two small fins to help with steering.

BIG EYES

Up to 27 cm (10.6 in) across, the giant squid's two eyes are probably the largest of any animal's. Their huge pupils (the holes through which light enters the eye) collect as much light as possible in the dim, deep water—more than 300 m (980 ft) below the surface—where this squid lives. This allows the squid to detect movements and shapes.

GIGANTIC CREATURE

Like many deep-sea animals, the giant squid is much larger than its shallow-water relatives. This characteristic is known as deep-sea gigantism. It is possibly caused by there being less prey in deeper, darker waters.

Larger animals have a better chance of catching what little prey there is. They can also swallow huge prey, allowing them to survive a long time before needing to feed again. Over time, these factors have caused deep-sea animals to evolve to be larger.

Sea Slugs and Snails

More than 30,000 species of slugs and snails live in the oceans. Slugs and snails are gastropods, meaning "stomach foot" in ancient Greek, because they crawl on a large, fleshy "foot" along their underside. Gastropods with a shell are often called snails, while the rest are called slugs.

GOLDEN NEMBROTHA

The golden nembrotha belongs to a group of sea slugs known as nudibranchs. It crawls across the seafloor, feeding on sessile invertebrates called sea squirts. It takes oxygen from the water through a plume of feather-like gills that extend from its back.

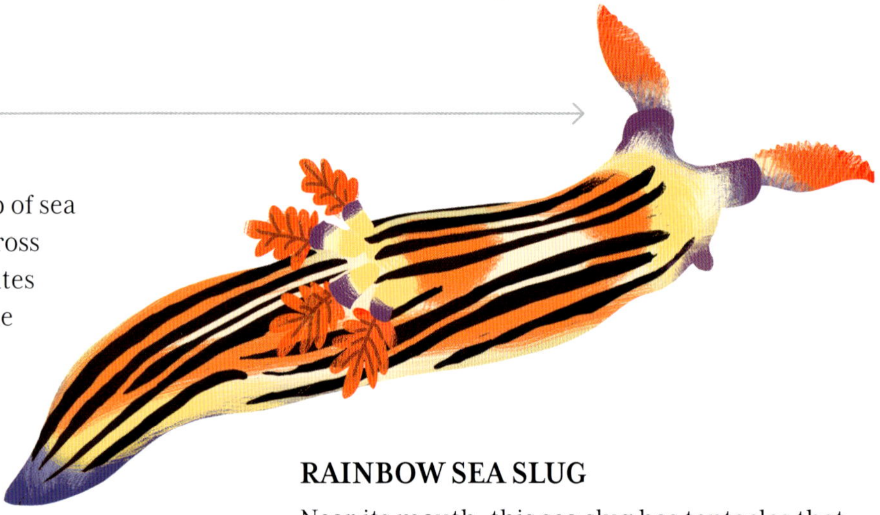

RAINBOW SEA SLUG

Near its mouth, this sea slug has tentacles that are sensitive to touch, taste, and smell. It also has tall leaf-shaped sense organs called rhinophores, which detect smell. Its tiny, basic eyes are at the base of the rhinophores. Oxygen is breathed through many finger-like organs, called cerata, which cover the slug's back.

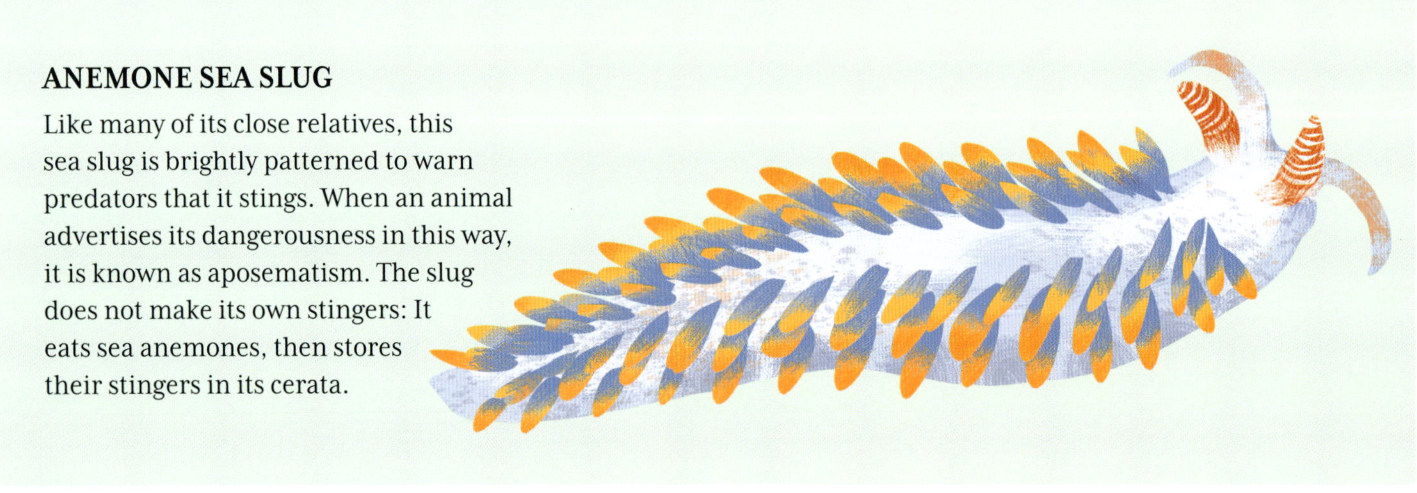

ANEMONE SEA SLUG

Like many of its close relatives, this sea slug is brightly patterned to warn predators that it stings. When an animal advertises its dangerousness in this way, it is known as aposematism. The slug does not make its own stingers: It eats sea anemones, then stores their stingers in its cerata.

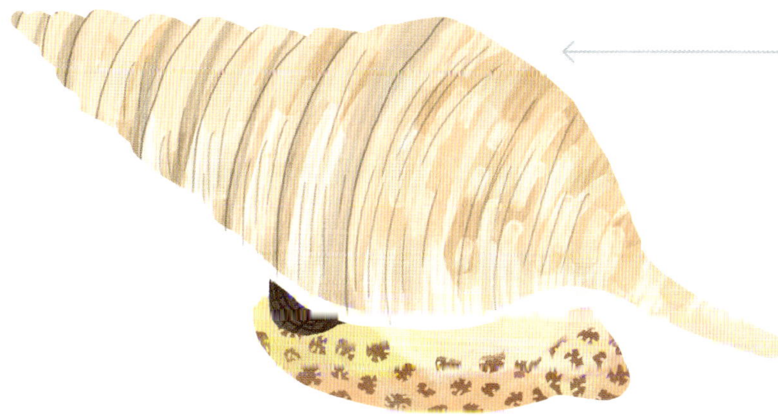

AUSTRALIAN TRUMPET SNAIL

With a shell up to 72 cm (28 in) long, this is the largest snail in the world. Like nearly all snails, it has a spiraling shell, into which it pulls its soft body for protection. As the snail grows, its builds more shell, adding more whorls to the spiral.

TEXTILE CONE

Named for its patterned, cone-shaped shell, this sea snail eats fish and other snails. Using a hard, needle-like tongue, called a radula, it injects its prey with venom. The snail, which lives in the Indian and Pacific Oceans, makes enough venom to kill several adult humans.

FLAMINGO TONGUE SNAIL

This snail covers its shell with a flap of brightly patterned, soft body tissue. This tissue is aposematic: It warns predators that the snail contains venom, which it has absorbed from the corals it eats. The snail feeds on soft corals by scraping with its rough radula.

Sea Slug and Snail Facts

CLASS	Gastropods
PHYLUM	Mollusks
SIZE	0.03–72 cm (0.01–28 in) long
RANGE	Intertidal zone, seafloor, and open water of all oceans
DIET	Algae, plants, and animals such as sponges, corals, fish, and snails

Around a Vent

On the deep ocean floor are hundreds of hydrothermal vents. These are cracks in the rock, from which water heated inside Earth's crust escapes. The water—which can reach over 60 °C (140 °F)—is rich in minerals, which can stick together and build up, making tall chimneys of rock.

A food chain is a series of living things that feed on each other. On land and in sunlit shallow water, many food chains begin with plants, which make their own food from sunlight. However, in the darkness around a deep-sea vent, most food chains start with tiny bacteria that make their own food from minerals pumped out by the vent.

Some bacteria are eaten by animals such as sea spiders, which are in turn eaten by bigger predatory animals such as shrimp and crabs. Other bacteria live inside the bodies of invertebrates such as mussels and worms, which share the food made by the bacteria. These are examples of symbiosis, which is when two species live together.

HYDROTHERMAL MUSSEL

Using its tube-like siphon, this mussel sucks in water and food particles, which are trapped by the mussel's gills. The particles include bacteria that set up home in the gills. The bacteria use minerals in the water to make their own food, some of which is soaked up by the mussel.

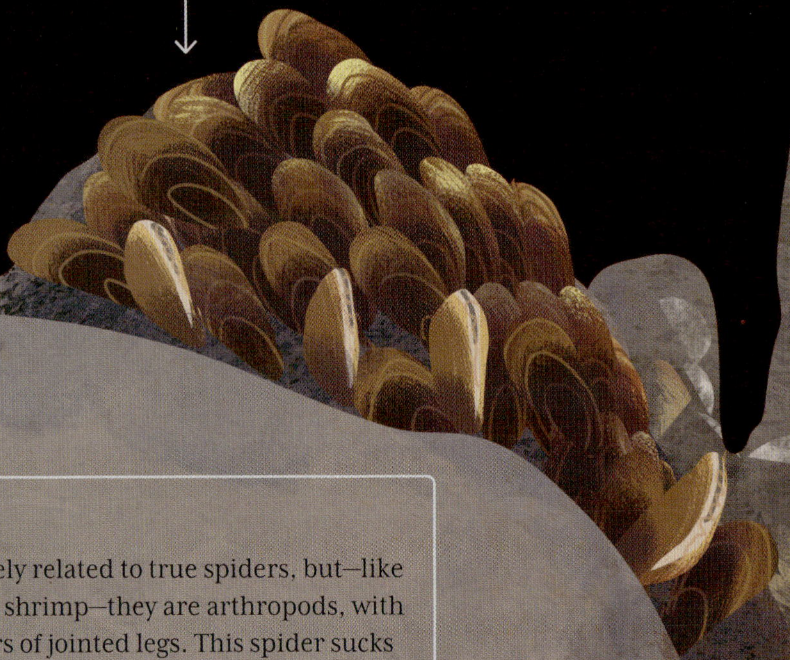

VENT SEA SPIDER

Sea spiders are not closely related to true spiders, but—like true spiders, crabs, and shrimp—they are arthropods, with an exoskeleton and pairs of jointed legs. This spider sucks up food, including bacteria and specks of dead animals, using a tube-like mouthpart called a proboscis.

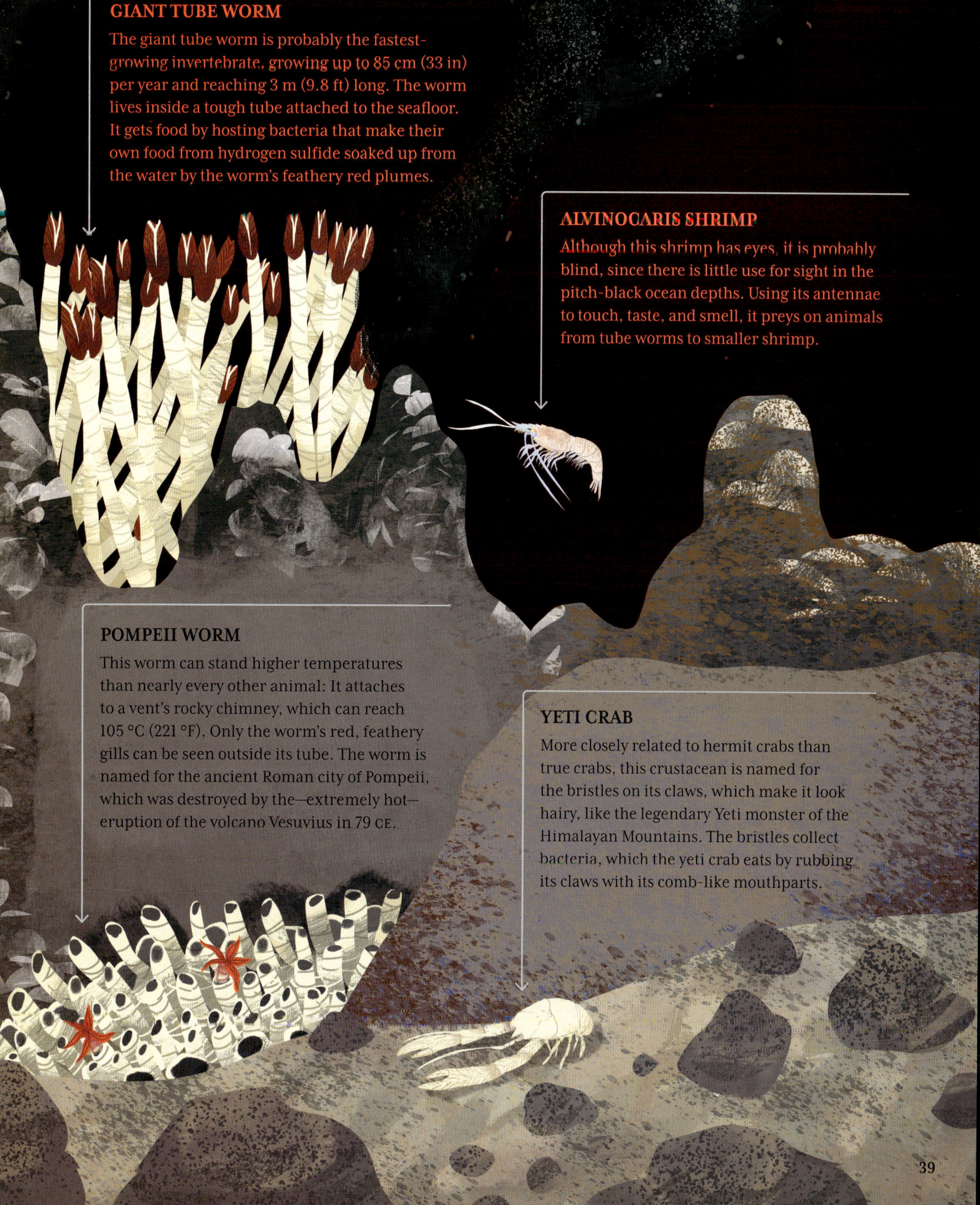

GIANT TUBE WORM

The giant tube worm is probably the fastest-growing invertebrate, growing up to 85 cm (33 in) per year and reaching 3 m (9.8 ft) long. The worm lives inside a tough tube attached to the seafloor. It gets food by hosting bacteria that make their own food from hydrogen sulfide soaked up from the water by the worm's feathery red plumes.

ALVINOCARIS SHRIMP

Although this shrimp has eyes, it is probably blind, since there is little use for sight in the pitch-black ocean depths. Using its antennae to touch, taste, and smell, it preys on animals from tube worms to smaller shrimp.

POMPEII WORM

This worm can stand higher temperatures than nearly every other animal: It attaches to a vent's rocky chimney, which can reach 105 °C (221 °F). Only the worm's red, feathery gills can be seen outside its tube. The worm is named for the ancient Roman city of Pompeii, which was destroyed by the—extremely hot—eruption of the volcano Vesuvius in 79 CE.

YETI CRAB

More closely related to hermit crabs than true crabs, this crustacean is named for the bristles on its claws, which make it look hairy, like the legendary Yeti monster of the Himalayan Mountains. The bristles collect bacteria, which the yeti crab eats by rubbing its claws with its comb-like mouthparts.

Headless Chicken Monster

This strangely named animal is a sea cucumber, a member of a group of invertebrates with a long, rounded body that often looks a little like a cucumber. There are more than 1,700 species of sea cucumbers, which usually spend all their time on the ocean floor. However, this sea cucumber is unusual because it has a more complex body shape—looking a little like a chicken without a head—and spends much of its time swimming or floating through the water.

THE CUCUMBER CLUB

Along with other sea cucumbers, the headless chicken monster is an echinoderm. The echinoderm group also includes sea urchins and starfish, which are also called sea stars. Echinoderms do not have a brain, but they do have nerves that react to touch, light, temperature, and water movements. While most echinoderms are protected by tough plates beneath their leathery skin, sea cucumbers have a softer body.

A DIFFERENT LIFE

The headless chicken monster eats the rotting remains of dead animals that have sunk to the seafloor. It uses its tentacles, which form a circle around its mouth, to pull the rotting material into its mouth, along with surrounding sand or mud. That unwanted sand and mud are expelled as poop through the anus, which is at the opposite end of the body from the mouth.

Unusually for a sea cucumber, the headless chicken has two sets of webbed, umbrella-like fins, one at the

The headless chicken monster has pinkish, transparent skin, which means we can see inside its body. The intestine, a tube that travels between the mouth and anus, is where food is broken down and soaked up.

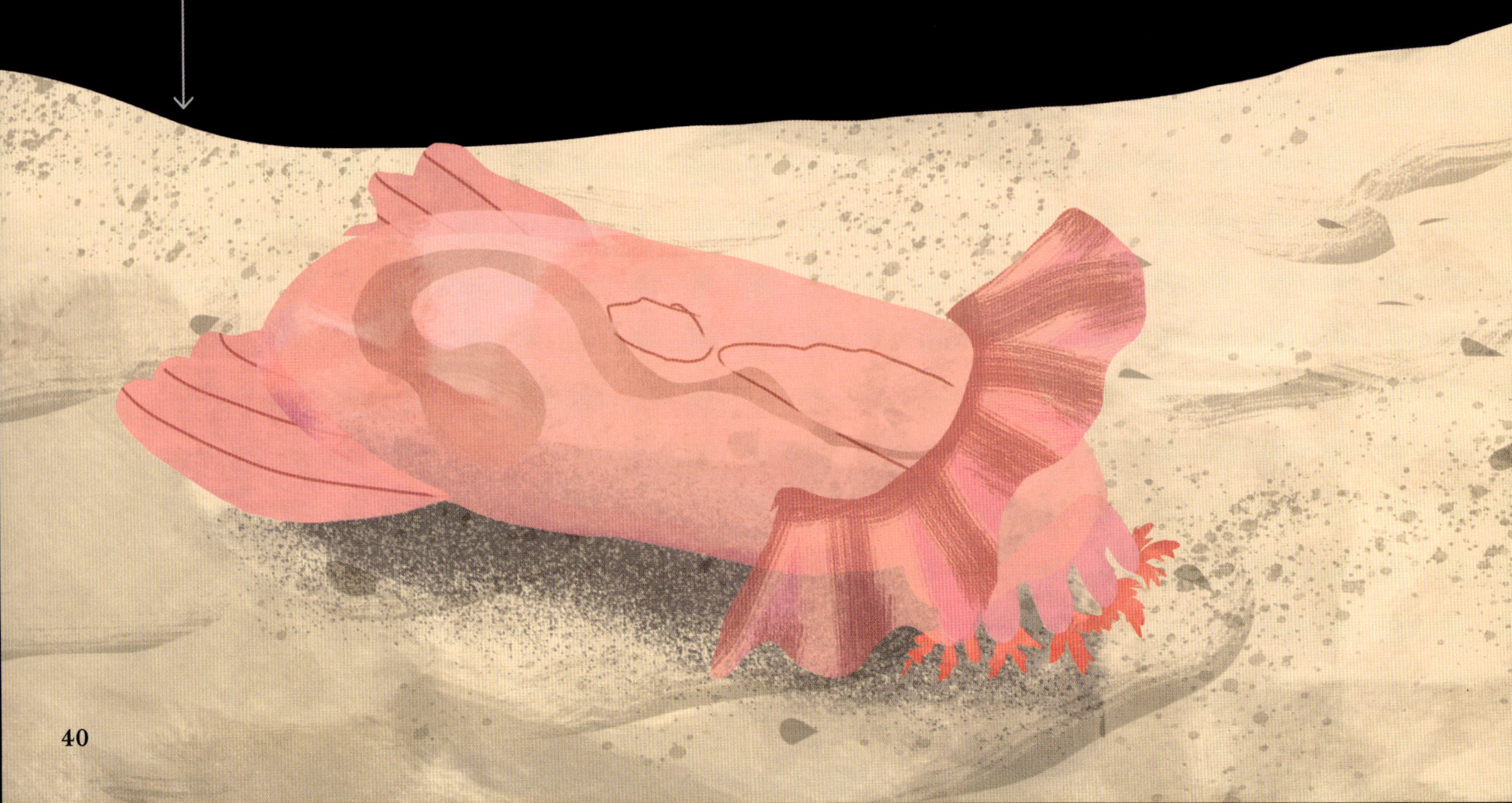

front and one at the back of its body. It spends only around a minute at a time feeding on the seafloor. Then it uses its fins and tentacles to push off the floor, floating as far as 1,000 m (3,300 ft) upward. Before launching off the bottom, the headless chicken often poops to reduce its weight. It then lets itself drift with the current or sink slowly back to the seafloor. This lifestyle helps the headless chicken to avoid seafloor-living predators as well as to find new feeding areas.

LIGHTING UP

Scientists have noticed that the headless chicken monster becomes bioluminescent if it is touched. Bioluminescence is when an animal gives off light. The cucumber's skin contains cells that give off light when triggered. This is probably a way for the cucumber to defend itself, as glowing flakes of skin drift away when the animal is rubbed. This distracts and confuses predators.

Chicken Monster Facts

SPECIES	*Enypniastes eximia*
CLASS	Sea cucumbers
PHYLUM	Echinoderms
SIZE	11–25 cm (4.3–10 in) long
RANGE	300–6,000 m (980–19,680 ft) deep in all oceans
DIET	Rotting material

Fish

There are more than 33,000 species of fish, around half of them living in the oceans rather than in freshwater rivers and lakes. One of the smallest fish is the male spinyhead seadevil, just 0.7 cm (0.3 in) long, while the largest is the whale shark, which grows to 18.8 m (61.7 ft). Fish can be found in all the ocean's habitats, from the icy waters of the Southern Ocean to the dark depths, where the abyssal cusk eel has been found 8,370 m (27,460 ft) below the surface.

Ocean fish belong to many different families and orders, all with different characteristics. The different body forms of fish are suited to their lifestyle and habitat. There are fast-swimming sharks, with skeletons made of lightweight, bendy cartilage rather than bone. Like other open-ocean fish, their bodies are streamlined, suited to cutting swiftly through the water in pursuit of prey and away from predators. In contrast, there are bony-plated seahorses, which spend most of their time motionless, their long tails curled around a coral stem or seagrass as they hide from predators. Then there are the flatfish, which lie on the seafloor as they wait for passing prey, their bodies flat and dappled in the browns of the ocean floor.

However, despite all these differences, most fish share some similarities: They usually have skin protected by small plates called scales, they have fins to help with swimming, and they take oxygen from the water using body parts called gills.

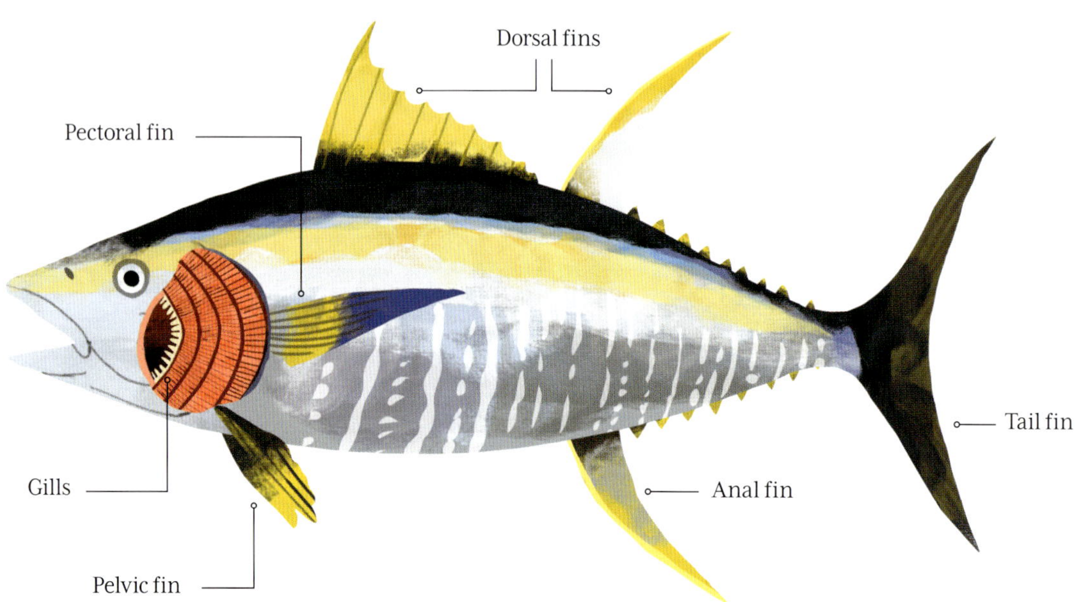

Like this yellowfin tuna, many fish have eight fins—two dorsal fins, two pectoral fins, two pelvic fins, an anal fin, and a tail fin—but some have more or fewer. Fins help with swimming, steering, and balance.

Water is gulped in through a fish's mouth, then passes through the gills (shown here in cutaway), where oxygen is soaked up by the blood. The used water flows out through gill slits, which are visible in sharks but hidden behind a bony cover in most fish.

Coral reefs are the busiest ocean habitats. More than 1,000 fish species are found on the coral reefs that surround the Indian Ocean's Maldives islands. Redtoothed triggerfish (left and bottom left) look for sponges. A daisy parrotfish (middle) uses its parrot-like beak to scrape up algae that grows on coral, while clown triggerfish (bottom right) hunt for small invertebrates.

Seahorses and Relatives

Seahorses, seadragons, and pipefish are not protected by scales but by thick, bony plates. This makes their body rigid, so they swim only by waving their fins rather than by wiggling their body, making them slower than most fish. They have a long snout with jaws that are fused together, forming a tube through which they suck food.

BARGIBANT'S PYGMY SEAHORSE

Less than 2 cm (0.8 in) long, this seahorse lives among gorgonian corals, where it anchors itself by curling its tail around a stem while it waits for invertebrates to pass. The seahorse is well camouflaged by its bumps, called tubercles, which match the shade of the gorgonian's polyps.

BIG-BELLY SEAHORSE

Like other male seahorses, the male big-belly has an egg pouch on his abdomen. To attract a female, the male inflates his pouch with water, blowing it up like a balloon. The female then squirts 300 to 700 eggs into the pouch, where they meet his sperm. When the eggs hatch, the male squeezes the newborns into the water.

HEDGEHOG SEAHORSE

This seahorse's dappled pattern—along with its frondy, spiny skin—breaks up its outline so it is difficult to spot among the corals and sponges of its reef habitat. The seahorse's exact shades, ranging from red and yellow to beige, depend on the corals it lives among.

LEAFY SEADRAGON

Unlike seahorses, which swim upright and have a grasping tail, seadragons swim horizontally and cannot grasp with their tail. Fertilized eggs are not stored in a pouch, but are stuck to the male's tail. However, like seahorses, seadragons are well camouflaged: Their skin grows leaflike flaps so the fish look like floating seaweed.

ALLIGATOR PIPEFISH

This pipefish lives among seaweed and in seagrass meadows, where it hides by positioning itself vertically, holding on with its grasping tail. A male alligator pipefish stores fertilized eggs in a pouch, like a male seahorse does, although some other male pipefish keep them on their tail.

ORNATE GHOST PIPEFISH

Floating motionlessly among sea lilies (pictured) or gorgonians, this pipefish sucks up shrimp through its tube-like snout. Unlike a true pipefish, a female ghost pipefish takes care of her own eggs—which are stuck to her pelvic fins—until they hatch.

Seahorse Facts

FAMILY	Seahorses, seadragons, and pipefish
ORDER	Syngnathiformes
SIZE	1.4–35 cm (0.6–13.8 in) long
RANGE	Shallow coastal waters of the Atlantic, Indian, and Pacific Oceans
DIET	Tiny invertebrates such as shrimp

Common Clownfish

This little fish lives among the stinging tentacles of sea anemones in what is called a symbiotic relationship. Symbiotic means "living together" in ancient Greek. It is a close, long-term relationship between two species. Some symbiotic relationships can be harmful to one species, but this relationship is very useful to both the clownfish and the anemone.

ANEMONE HOME

This clownfish lives in three species of sea anemones: the magnificent (pictured), giant carpet, and Merten's carpet. Anemones are invertebrates that catch prey such as small fish by stinging with the tentacles that surround the anemone's central mouth. A common clownfish is covered in thick mucus that protects it from these stings. By hiding among an anemone's tentacles, the clownfish has protection from predators. It can feed on tiny invertebrates that float past in the current, as well as bits of the anemone's food that escape from its mouth.

The sea anemone also benefits from the relationship. Its clownfish feed on parasites that settle on the tentacles, keeping them healthy. The presence of the bright clownfish may attract predator fish to the anemone, so the anemone can feed on them. Finally, the clownfish's poop gives nutrients to the anemone.

LIVING TOGETHER

A group of common clownfish lives together in an anemone. Within each group, there is a larger, dominant female, who controls the group; the large male that she mates with; then around four smaller male clownfish who do not mate. All common clownfish are born male, but the largest male in each anemone turns into a female. When that female dies, the next largest male turns into a female.

GROWING UP

At mating time, the group's big male chases the female to a nest area on a nearby rock, hidden by tentacles. The female lays more than 600 sticky eggs, then the male fertilizes them and watches over them, fanning them with his fins so they get the oxygen they need to develop.

After around a week, the eggs hatch into tiny non-swimming larvae, which drift away in the current. Over the next days and weeks, the larvae develop and grow fins, until they have their adult form. Now a young, male clownfish needs to find an anemone. He may visit several anemones before he finds a female willing to accept him as the new, smallest member of the group.

Clownfish in a group can communicate with each other by making clicking, popping, and tooth-grinding noises.

Common Clownfish Facts

SPECIES	*Amphiprion ocellaris*
SUBFAMILY	Clownfish and damselfish
CLADE	Percomorpha
SIZE	6–11 cm (2.4–4.3 in) long
RANGE	Sea anemones in shallow coastal water of the Indian and Pacific Oceans
DIET	Zooplankton and algae

On a Coral Reef

In the Pacific Ocean, the islands of Hawaii are ringed by coral reefs, which thrive in the warm, shallow, sunlit water. The reefs are home to more than 400 species of fish. Some eat the corals or shelter among them, while others—such as sharks—prey on those that do.

Many reef fish have a laterally compressed body, which means it is narrow from side to side. This body shape allows them to swim through narrow gaps in the reef, but also helps them change direction quickly with a flick of the body and tail. In contrast, fish that swim in open, obstacle-free water have a streamlined body that is roughly cylinder-shaped but narrower at front and back, so they can cut through the water at speed.

Reef fish often have bright, patterned bodies, which helps with camouflage on the reef, among vivid coral and the dappled patterns of sunlight and shade. Strongly contrasting stripes or spots also make it difficult for a predator to make out the clear outline of a fish. In addition, bright patterns help these fish at mating time, when they need to spot other members of their species among all the fish on the busy reef.

MOORISH IDOL

This fish has a small mouth with bristle-like teeth, which it uses for scraping at corals and sponges. Its long, trailing dorsal fin is shown off to attract a mate, as it is a sign of health. A short dorsal fin is a sign of weakness, as it means that predators have nibbled the fin.

ACHILLES TANG

On either side of its tail, this fish has a knife-like spine, which is folded against the body when swimming—but is flicked outward if the tang is attacked. The spine can give a deep wound. The tang feeds on algae that grow on the coral.

SCALLOPED HAMMERHEAD SHARK

This shark is named for its hammer-shaped head, which has a ruffled front edge. With an eye at either end of the hammer, the shark can see above, below, and all around. However, it cannot see directly ahead, so it turns its head side to side as it searches for fish and squid.

SADDLE BUTTERFLYFISH

The large black spot on this fish's back is an example of "disruptive coloration": when an animal's pattern makes it hard to see where the fish begins and the water ends. This butterflyfish feeds on algae, coral, and eggs that have been laid in crevices.

RUSSET ANGELFISH

When a male and female angelfish are ready to mate, they swim close to each other. The female releases hundreds of eggs, and the male releases his sperm into the water. The fertilized eggs float freely in the water until they hatch, but many become food for predators.

WHITESADDLE GOATFISH

Found only around Hawaii, this goatfish has two fronds, called barbels, on its chin, a little bit like a goat's "beard." The barbels are sensitive to touch and smells. The fish uses them to search the sand for worms and shrimp.

Yellowhead Jawfish

This fish is a mouthbrooder, which means that a parent—in this case, the father—holds developing eggs in its mouth. This strategy helps to prevent the eggs being eaten by predators. This means that yellowhead jawfish can produce fewer eggs than most fish, which usually give their many eggs no protection at all.

FISHY METHODS

Fish have different methods of producing babies. In around 3 percent of fish—including sharks such as the hammerhead—females give birth to live young after mating. The newborn fish, which get no care from their parents, are fairly large and able to swim and feed.

Most other female fish release eggs into the water, where they are fertilized by sperm released by a male. Then both parents swim away. Usually, many hundreds or thousands of eggs are produced. The ocean sunfish produces the most: up to 300 million in one season. With so many eggs, a few will probably—despite the risks—hatch into larvae, then survive long enough to develop into adult fish.

Around 10 percent of fish have another strategy, including sticklebacks, which lay eggs in nests that are closely guarded; seahorses, which store fertilized eggs in the male's pouch until hatching; and mouthbrooders such as the jawfish. While male jawfish do the mouthbrooding, in some fish species, such as African cichlids, it is females that do so.

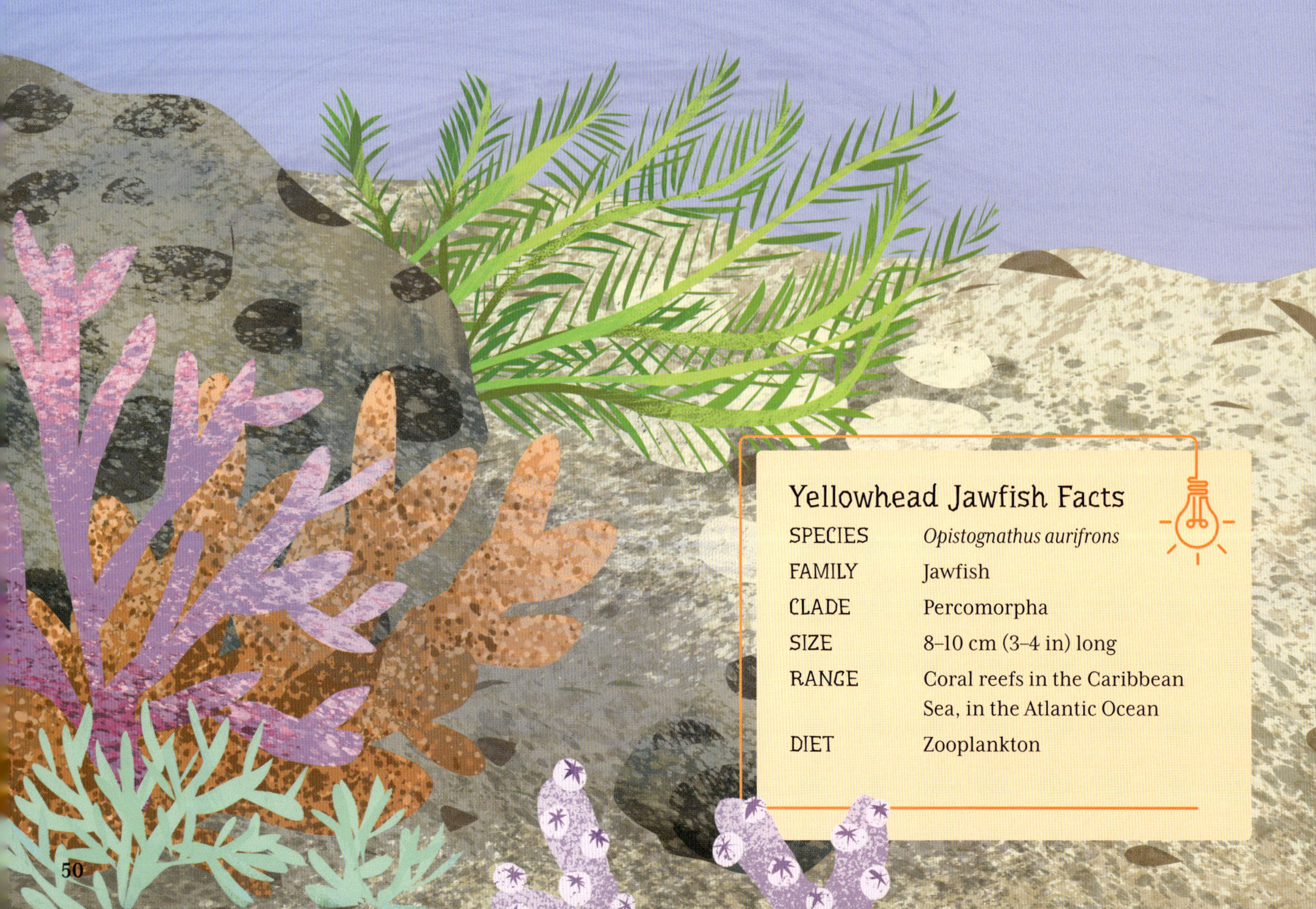

Yellowhead Jawfish Facts

SPECIES	*Opistognathus aurifrons*
FAMILY	Jawfish
CLADE	Percomorpha
SIZE	8–10 cm (3–4 in) long
RANGE	Coral reefs in the Caribbean Sea, in the Atlantic Ocean
DIET	Zooplankton

BIG MOUTH

Compared with its body size, the yellowhead jawfish has a large head and mouth. Holding eggs is not the only use for this mouth. The jawfish spends much of its time in a burrow that it digs in the sandy seafloor, by taking mouthfuls of sand then spitting them out elsewhere. The jawfish often hovers with its upper body sticking out of its burrow, as it waits for tiny invertebrates to drift by so it can snap them up. When it senses a predator, the fish sinks into its burrow.

At mating time, the male attracts a female by darting in and out of his burrow. Eventually, a female lays around 400 eggs in the male's burrow, where they are fertilized by the male. Then the male gathers the eggs into his mouth. While he broods the eggs, he cannot eat. When the eggs hatch after around 5 days—and the larvae float away—the male is hungry and underweight.

Every so often, a male yellowhead jawfish opens his mouth, pushes the eggs partway out, and turns them. This allows all the eggs to soak up oxygen from the water, which they need for development.

Wrasses

There are more than 600 species of wrasses, which usually live in shallow, warm water. Wrasses have thick lips and protrusible mouths, which means that they can shoot forward their jaws to catch prey. Many wrasse species are also able to change sex.

SLING-JAW WRASSE

This fish has the most extremely protrusible mouth of any wrasse: It can spring forward its jaws by up to half its body length. This not only allows the wrasse to extend its reach, but also creates a vacuum, as the fish's suddenly enlarged mouth is empty. Water—containing small fish—rushes in to fill the space, just like air and dust rush into a vacuum cleaner.

HUMPHEAD WRASSE

The largest wrasse, the humphead is up to 2 m (6.6 ft) long and lives for around 30 years. All humpheads are born female, but the largest females become male at around 9 years old. This strategy has probably evolved because small males are stopped from mating with females by larger males, so it is better to become a male only when big.

BIRD WRASSE

The bird wrasse is named for its snout, which is a little like a bird's beak. The snout is used to reach small invertebrates in the crevices of coral reefs. As a bird wrasse changes from female to male, it also changes pattern: from black, white, and red, to green and yellow.

SIX-LINE WRASSE

This wrasse has an eye-like marking, called an eyespot, on its tail. This confuses predators, which prefer to catch fish from the head end, so that their prey's spiny fins do not get stuck while being swallowed. At night, this wrasse sleeps in a coral crevice in a bubble of its own mucus, which stops predators from smelling it.

BLUESTREAK CLEANER WRASSE

The bluestreak eats parasites and dead tissue from the skin of bigger fish, such as this grouper. This keeps the big fish healthy, while the bluestreak is protected from predators by the big fish's presence. The bluestreak waits for clients at a particular spot on its coral reef, called a cleaning station.

MOON WRASSE

Named for the yellow, moonlike marking on an adult's tail, this wrasse changes from female to male when it reaches 11 cm (4.3 in) long. The change takes 10 days, as the body stops making eggs and starts to make sperm.

Wrasse Facts

FAMILY	Wrasses
ORDER	Labriformes
SIZE	5–200 cm (2–79 in) long
RANGE	Shallow coastal waters of the Atlantic, Indian, and Pacific Oceans
DIET	Fish, invertebrates, and dead fish skin

Mandarinfish

This fish is named for its bright pattern, which looks like the beautiful robes worn by medieval Chinese officials called mandarins. The mandarinfish swims and hovers by whirring its pectoral fins. It can also walk across the seafloor on its large pelvic fins as it looks for worms to snap up with its small mouth.

SMELLY FISH

Unlike most fish, mandarinfish do not have scales to protect their skin. Instead, their skin makes thick mucus for protection. The skin also makes a chemical that smells and tastes awful, which makes predators not want to eat mandarinfish. The fish's vivid pattern is aposematic: It warns predators, such as scorpionfish, that the fish tastes awful. If a predator once tastes the mandarinfish, the pattern will help it remember never to do so again.

The mandarinfish gives itself further protection by hunting only at night. To help with seeing in dim light conditions, it has huge eyes. During the day, it hides under corals, between the branches of staghorn corals, or burrows into sand, leaving only its eyes above the surface.

DANCING TOGETHER

Male and female mandarinfish look different: The male is larger and has a long spine on its first dorsal fin. Mandarinfish mate frequently, at any time of year. Just before sunset, females gather in small groups on the reef. Males visit different groups until they find a willing female. To win over a female, males spread and display their fins, while opening and closing their mouths. A female is more likely to choose a bigger, stronger-looking male, with longer fins and brighter skin.

Males often become aggressive with each other when trying to mate. Fights can break out, with males biting and tussling each other. Some males die from their injuries, resulting in there being slightly more adult females than males.

When a mating pair have chosen each other, they swim upward, pressed closely together, rising around 1 m (3.3 ft) above the reef. The female releases around 200 eggs, and the male releases his sperm. Then the pair separate, leaving their fertilized eggs behind. The eggs float away in the current.

Mandarinfish Facts

SPECIES	*Synchiropus splendidus*
FAMILY	Dragonets
ORDER	Callionymiformes
SIZE	5–7 cm (2–2.8 in) long
RANGE	Coral reefs in the Pacific Ocean
DIET	Fish eggs and small invertebrates such as worms and seed shrimp

A female mandarinfish (left) mates just once a night, but a male may mate with several females. The female will mate again after a few days, when she has made more eggs. Such frequent mating ensures that enough eggs will survive to adulthood to keep the total number of mandarinfish stable.

In the Mangroves

Mangrove trees and bushes grow along warm coasts, in the intertidal zone, which is covered by water at high tide and exposed at low tide. One of India's largest mangrove forests, covering 45 sq km (17 sq miles) is at Pichavaram, in the country's southeast.

Unlike most plants, which cannot tolerate salt, mangroves can grow in salty water because their roots have evolved to filter out as much as 90 percent of the salt found in seawater. Mangrove leaves also have a waxy coating, which stops them from losing too much fresh water, so they can limit the salt water they need to take in through their roots.

Mangroves have long, stilt-like roots that keep their leaves above the water level. The roots provide a sheltered spot for many fish to lay eggs, where larger predators cannot reach them. After hatching, countless young fish stay among the mangroves until adulthood, when they swim out to sea. Many others stay in this food-rich habitat throughout their life.

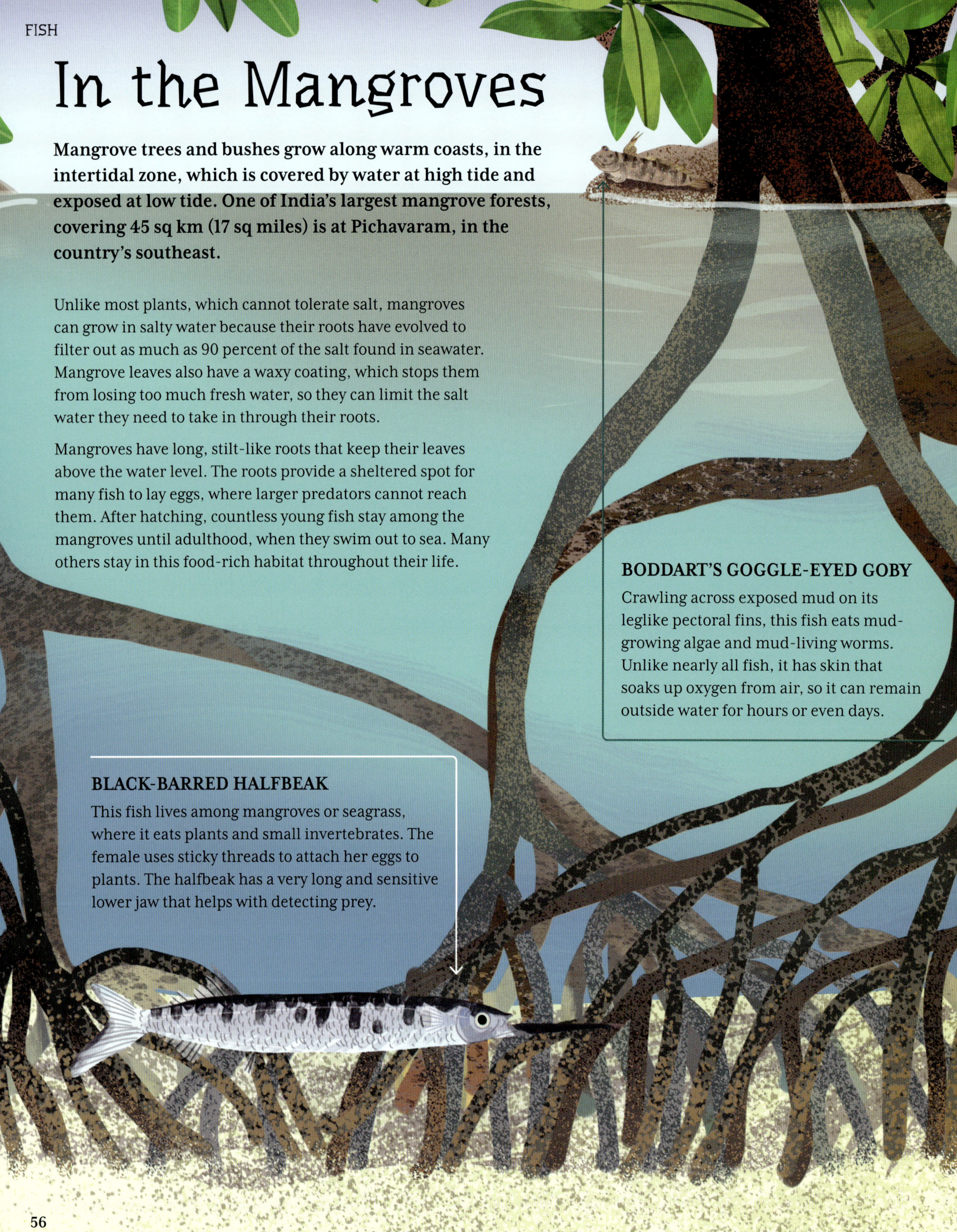

BODDART'S GOGGLE-EYED GOBY

Crawling across exposed mud on its leglike pectoral fins, this fish eats mud-growing algae and mud-living worms. Unlike nearly all fish, it has skin that soaks up oxygen from air, so it can remain outside water for hours or even days.

BLACK-BARRED HALFBEAK

This fish lives among mangroves or seagrass, where it eats plants and small invertebrates. The female uses sticky threads to attach her eggs to plants. The halfbeak has a very long and sensitive lower jaw that helps with detecting prey.

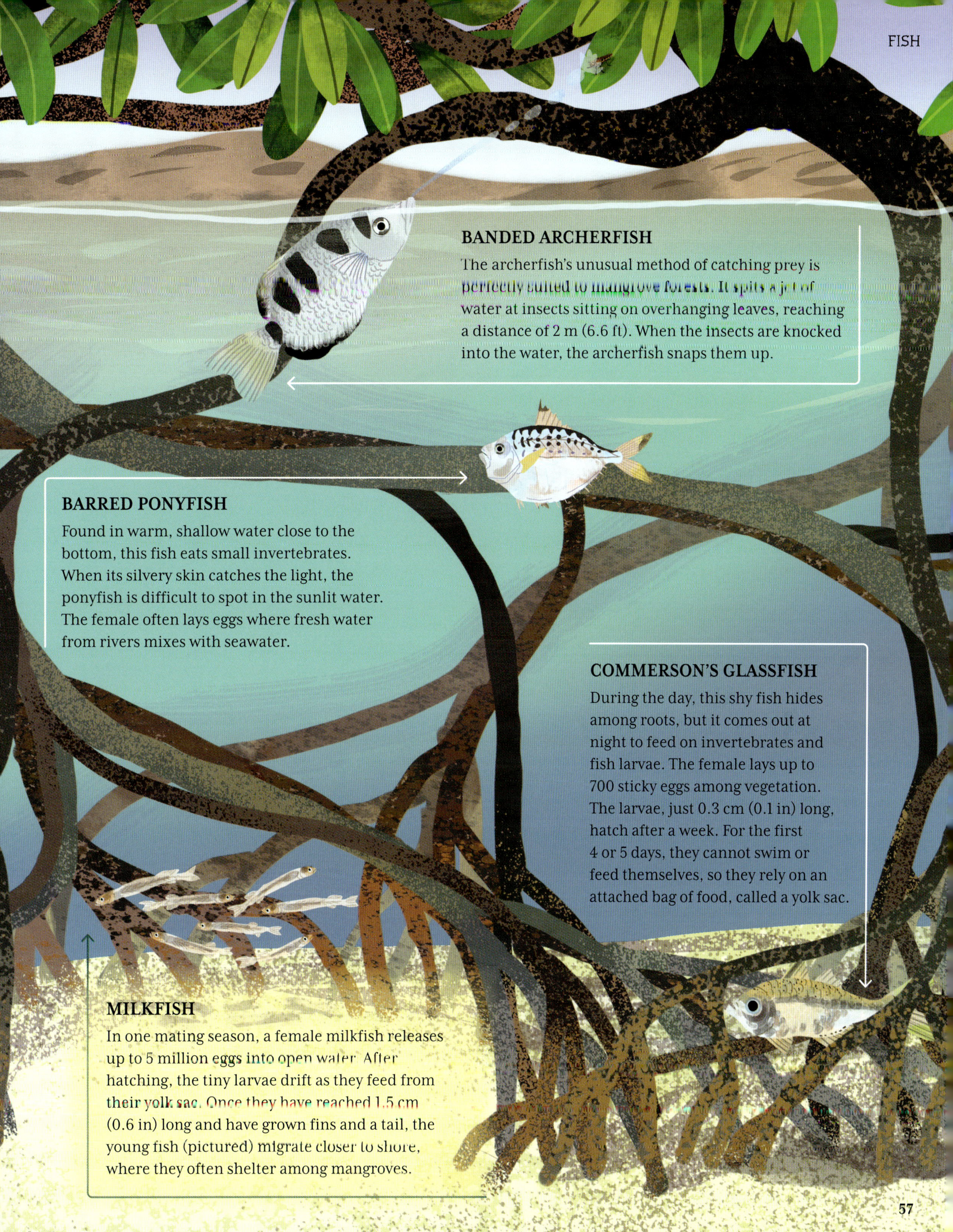

BANDED ARCHERFISH

The archerfish's unusual method of catching prey is perfectly suited to mangrove forests. It spits a jet of water at insects sitting on overhanging leaves, reaching a distance of 2 m (6.6 ft). When the insects are knocked into the water, the archerfish snaps them up.

BARRED PONYFISH

Found in warm, shallow water close to the bottom, this fish eats small invertebrates. When its silvery skin catches the light, the ponyfish is difficult to spot in the sunlit water. The female often lays eggs where fresh water from rivers mixes with seawater.

COMMERSON'S GLASSFISH

During the day, this shy fish hides among roots, but it comes out at night to feed on invertebrates and fish larvae. The female lays up to 700 sticky eggs among vegetation. The larvae, just 0.3 cm (0.1 in) long, hatch after a week. For the first 4 or 5 days, they cannot swim or feed themselves, so they rely on an attached bag of food, called a yolk sac.

MILKFISH

In one mating season, a female milkfish releases up to 5 million eggs into open water. After hatching, the tiny larvae drift as they feed from their yolk sac. Once they have reached 1.5 cm (0.6 in) long and have grown fins and a tail, the young fish (pictured) migrate closer to shore, where they often shelter among mangroves.

Scorpionfish

This family contains some of the world's most venomous species. To protect themselves, scorpionfish inject attackers with venom by pricking with their sharp spines, which contain venom-making glands. There are over 450 scorpionfish species, many of them living on coral reefs.

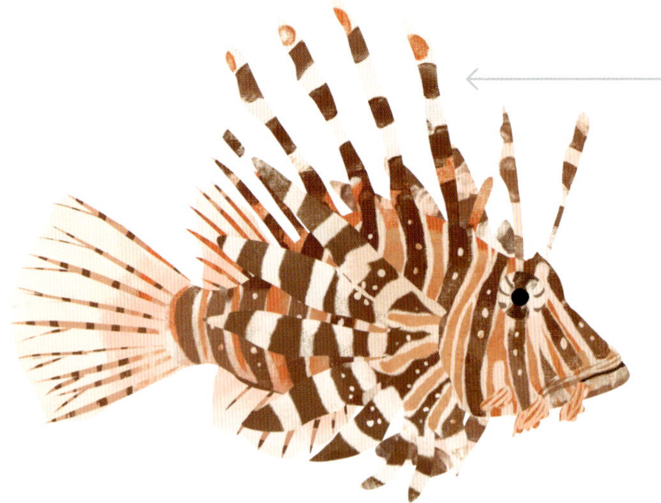

RED LIONFISH

This slow-swimming fish uses its painful venom to kill or stun attackers. It has 13 venomous spines in its dorsal fin, 1 in each of its pelvic fins, and 3 in its anal fin. Along with its other, fanlike, non-venomous fins, these spines look a little bit like a lion's mane.

TWOSPOT TURKEYFISH

Sheltering in crevices during the day, this fish hunts for small fish and invertebrates at night. It uses the fleshy threads on its lower jaw, called barbels, to attract prey, which mistake them for small fish or worms. The two eyespots on the fish's dorsal fin may frighten away predators, because they seem to be the eyes of a larger animal.

WEEDY SCORPIONFISH

This scorpionfish is covered in weedlike fronds of skin, which make it look like a coral or feather duster worm. This camouflage allows the fish to creep up on prey by shuffling across the seafloor on its fins. Then it opens its mouth and sucks in prey, swallowing it whole.

TASSELED SCORPIONFISH

Its brown-orange pattern and skin tassels help this scorpionfish to go unnoticed as it lies among corals. With 15 venomous spines, spread between its dorsal and anal fins, this seafloor-living scorpionfish can give a painful sting to the feet of unwary swimmers.

COCKATOO WASPFISH

With its dorsal fin rising from the top of its head, this fish appears to have a crest like the parrots called cockatoos. It sucks in small shrimp that pass near its mouth as it lies on the seafloor, swaying in the current like a fan coral or dead leaf.

HORRID STONEFISH

Although it looks like a stone as it lies on the seafloor, partly buried by sand, this is one of the world's most venomous fish. It raises its spines if disturbed by a predator or human. The venom affects human hearts and muscles, but on coasts where the fish is common—from Japan to Australia—medicine is available for treatment.

Scorpionfish Facts

FAMILY	Scorpionfish
ORDER	Scorpaeniformes
SIZE	5–108 cm (2–43 in) long
RANGE	Shallow coastal waters of the Atlantic, Indian, and Pacific Oceans
DIET	Fish and invertebrates such as snails and shrimp

White-Spotted Puffer

The white-spotted puffer is a slow swimmer. It has a rigid, unbending body, so it swims only by waving its fins rather than by wriggling its body as many other fish do. To make up for this lack of speed, the white-spotted puffer has an extraordinary way to defend itself: It inflates its body like a balloon, making itself too big for predators to swallow.

PUFFING UP

The puffer has an extremely stretchy stomach. If it is attacked by a predator, it gulps in water, filling its stomach until its body is almost round. The puffer also has many pointed spines. When the fish is bloated with water, these stick out in all directions. Most predators now find the puffer too large and prickly to eat. If they try to swallow it, the puffer may stick in their throat and choke them.

MAKING POISON

If a predator manages to eat the puffer, they will find that it tastes awful—and may be deadly. A powerful chemical, called tetrodotoxin, is found in the puffer's organs, including its intestines, liver, and skin.

Tetrodotoxin quickly affects the predator's nerves, blocking signals between the brain and muscles. For smaller predators, this causes paralysis (inability to move), which causes suffocation since the lungs cannot work.

Scientists think that the puffer gets its tetrodotoxin from bacteria that live in the shellfish it eats. The bacteria set up home in the puffer's intestines. The puffer has evolved to be unaffected by the chemical. Females even wipe tetrodotoxin on their eggs, so that predators do not want to eat them.

A puffer can double its size (right) by taking large gulps of water if it is surprised by a predator, such as a grouper (far right). The puffer swallows around 37 gulps in as little as 14 seconds. Deflating itself takes about twice as long.

Larger predators of the puffer, such as great white sharks, may not be killed by the tetrodotoxin, but they are likely to remember the unpleasant taste and feelings. In the future, they will leave white-spotted puffers alone. The puffer's pattern of spots, with startling circles around its eyes, may be an example of aposematism, when an easy-to-remember pattern warns predators that an animal is bad to eat.

BITING HARD

The bones of the puffer's jaw form a beak, a little like a bird's. At both the top and bottom of the beak are two large teeth, making four teeth in total. Helped by very powerful jaw muscles, the teeth are used for cracking the hard shells of mollusks such as mussels and snails, as well as crustaceans including crabs. The teeth grow continuously, but are worn down by biting on hard foods.

White-Spotted Puffer Facts

SPECIES	*Arothron hispidus*
FAMILY	Puffers
ORDER	Tetraodontiformes
SIZE	40–50 cm (16–20 in) long
RANGE	Coastal waters of the Indian and Pacific Oceans
DIET	Algae, invertebrates such as snails, mussels, and coral, and small fish

On the Seafloor

Fish that live on or near the seafloor are known as demersal, which means "sinking" in Latin. On the coastal seafloor of the western Pacific Ocean, many demersal species are well camouflaged, so they are almost invisible among the sand and rocks.

While some demersal fish swim near the seafloor as they hunt for prey, many are ambush predators: They wait for passing prey. As they wait, these fish are camouflaged by their dappled patterns. Some, such as the leopard flounder, also bury themselves in sand or mud. Many ambushers have an upward-pointing mouth, ready to seize prey that swims overhead.

Many demersal fish do not have a swim bladder, a gas-filled sac that allows most fish to control their position in the water. As a result, many demersal fish are slightly heavier than water, so they can lie still on the seafloor. These bottom-resters usually have a flattened lower body. In contrast, the flatfish—a large group of demersal fish that includes flounders and sanddabs—are flattened from side to side, so they lie on their side.

FLASHER SANDGOBY

Just 5 cm (2 in) long, the flasher sandgoby has a translucent (see-through) body, making it difficult for predators or prey to spot. However, it has reddish eyes and a red patch on its first dorsal fin, which it flicks up and down to attract a mate.

DE BEAUFORT'S FLATHEAD

With its body dappled in creams and browns, this fish is almost invisible as it lies motionless on the seafloor. It has a flap of frondy tissue over each of its large black eyes, which helps to disguise them as they watch for small fish and crustaceans.

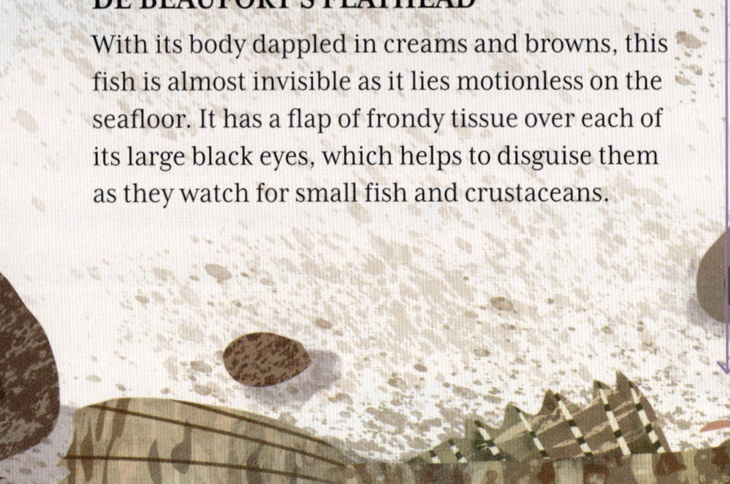

SPECKLED SANDPERCH

Propped on its pelvic fins, this ambush predator looks out for small invertebrates. Its large eyes are positioned high and facing to the sides, so it can see above and all around. The large eyespot on the sandperch's tail is protection against its own predators.

LEOPARD FLOUNDER

This flatfish started life with an eye on either side of its head, but its right eye moved to the left side as the fish took its adult form. This means the flounder can use both eyes as it lies on its right side on the seafloor. The flounder changes its skin pattern to blend in with sand and pebbles, by releasing skin pigments that make it darker or lighter.

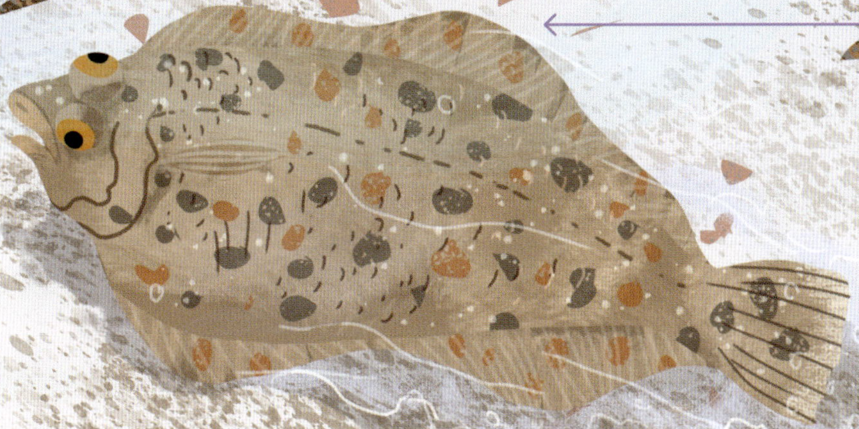

PACIFIC SANDDAB

The sanddab has both eyes on the left side of its head. These eyes are protrusible, which means they can be raised to see all around. Like other flatfish, the sanddab has a single dorsal fin that extends onto its head. The fish swims with its left side uppermost, using waves of its long dorsal and anal fins.

SLENDER GIANT MORAY

Up to 3.9 m (12.8 ft) long, this eel has a wide mouth with two sets of biting jaws: An extra, movable set of jaws is in its throat. When feeding on prey such as fish and octopuses, the eel slides forward the second set to help grab prey, then slides them back to carry prey into the throat.

Cartilaginous Fish

Unlike most fish, these fish have a skeleton made of lightweight, bendy cartilage rather than bone. This makes it easier for them to twist, turn, and swim fast. There are more than 1,000 species of cartilaginous fish, including sharks, rays, and chimaeras.

WHALE SHARK

Up to 18.8 m (61.7 ft) long, this is the largest of the more than 500 species of sharks—and also the world's largest fish. It feeds by gulping water containing tiny animals such as krill. Food is filtered from the water by sieve-like pads in the shark's mouth, in front of its gills, through which used water flows out.

BULL SHARK

This shark is named for being broad-bodied and aggressive, like a bull. Up to 3.5 m (11.5 ft) long, it feeds on fish, turtles, birds, and dolphins. At any time, it has up to 350 teeth in its mouth, which are replaced when they fall out. Over the shark's 20-year life, it may have 20,000 teeth.

PUFFADDER SHYSHARK

Living on or near the seafloor along the coast of South Africa, this small shark catches crabs and worms. It is named for its "shy" habit of curling up, with its tail covering its eyes, if it is frightened by a bigger fish. This helps the shark blend in among coral and rocks.

SMALLTOOTH SAWFISH

This fish is a ray, a group of cartilaginous fish with wide, flattened bodies. The sawfish has a long, sawlike snout, with toothlike scales along each edge. The well-camouflaged sawfish lies on the seafloor as it waits for fish to swim overhead—then swipes with its saw.

GIANT MANTA RAY

This ray can grow 7 m (23 ft) wide, from the tip of one triangular pectoral fin to the other. It swims by flapping these fins, rather like a bird. On either side of the ray's mouth are finger-like body parts called cephalic fins. The ray curls these fins to funnel water containing small animals into its mouth.

RABBITFISH

Like other chimaeras, the rabbitfish has a whip-like tail and a venomous spine at the front of its first dorsal fin, which is protection from predators such as sharks. It has large eyes for seeing in the deep ocean. Its rubbery skin has no scales.

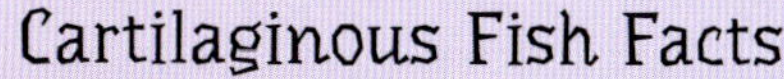

Cartilaginous Fish Facts

CLASS	Cartilaginous fish
INFRAPHYLUM	Vertebrates with jaws
SIZE	0.08–18.8 m (0.3–61.7 ft) long
RANGE	All oceans
DIET	Invertebrates, fish, reptiles, birds, and mammals

Great White Shark

This shark is the world's largest predatory fish. Although there are bigger fish—such as the whale shark and basking shark—those fish are filter-feeders, which sieve tiny creatures from the water. The great white is responsible for more bites to humans than any other shark, but attacks are extremely rare, because the shark prefers fattier prey, such as seals and sea lions.

SHARK ATTACK

The great white usually hunts alone, although it may gather in groups at feeding and mating areas. The shark often attacks prey that is swimming on or near the water surface, rushing upward to seize its victim at speeds of up to 25 km/h (16 miles per hour). As the shark lunges, it rolls its eyeballs backward in their sockets, so they are not damaged by thrashing prey.

The great white has around 50 rows of jagged-edged teeth, each row containing up to 7 teeth, one behind the other. At any one time, the shark has around 300 teeth in its mouth. When a front tooth falls out, as they frequently do when biting, the teeth behind move forward. When killing large prey, such as a seal or dolphin, the shark shakes its head from side to side so its teeth's jagged edges can saw into the animal's flesh.

SPECIAL SENSES

The shark has the same five senses as humans—sight, hearing, touch, taste, and smell—but its most powerful sense is smell. It can smell prey at a distance of up to 500 m (1,640 ft). Almost one-fifth of the great white's brain is dedicated to identifying smells. Tiny smell particles float from prey and into the shark's nostrils. The shark can figure out the direction of prey by the time at which the smell reaches each nostril.

Like all fish, the great white can also sense pressure changes in the water. A line of tiny dips, called pores, runs from its snout to its tail. Called the lateral line, these pores contain cells that react to water movement, caused by moving prey or by water rippling off the seabed.

Like most cartilaginous fish, the great white also has a sense called electroreception. On its head are pores, called ampullae of Lorenzini, that contain cells that detect electric fields. As all animals move, their muscles create tiny electric fields. The great white's electroreception allows it to sense moving prey, as well as the beating heart of a motionless animal that is close by.

Great White Shark Facts

SPECIES	*Carcharodon carcharias*
ORDER	Mackerel sharks
CLASS	Cartilaginous fish
SIZE	3.4–5.8 m (11.2–19 ft) long
RANGE	Atlantic, Indian, and Pacific Oceans
DIET	Seals, dolphins, whales, birds, turtles, squid, and fish including sharks

The great white has a form of camouflage called countershading: a dark back and a paler underside. Prey swimming at the water surface finds it difficult to see the shark's back in the dark water below. Yet prey swimming under the shark finds it difficult to see the shark's pale belly against the sunlight.

In the Open Ocean

In the surface waters of the Pacific Ocean, swordfish attack while sauries seek safety in their shoal. During the day, the upper 200 m (660 ft) of the water is lit by sunlight. Fish that live in this sunlit region of the open ocean, neither close to land nor the seafloor, are called epipelagic (from the ancient Greek for "near the surface").

Most epipelagic fish are in two groups: small schooling fish and the large predatory fish that hunt them. When a group of fish, called a shoal, swims together in the same direction, it is known as schooling. This gives some protection from predators: There are many eyes to keep watch, while each individual fish has a smaller chance of being eaten. Many schooling epipelagic fish are filter feeders, sieving tiny floating animals from the water.

Most epipelagic fish share some characteristics, whether they are predators or schoolers. They have a streamlined, flexible body with a powerful tail, allowing then to swim at speed and for long distances. Many epipelagic fish have shiny, silvery scales. Each scale acts as a tiny mirror, making the fish difficult to spot in the sunlit water.

CHUB MACKEREL

This fish swims in a shoal that may contain many thousands of fish. When swimming near the surface, where the mackerel feeds on zooplankton, the rippling pattern on the fish's upper back makes it difficult for seabirds to spot among the sunlit waves.

SWORDFISH

The swordfish has a long, flat upper jaw, forming a sword-like beak. The "sword" is slashed at fish and squid, so the startled or injured prey is easier to catch. With its large, smoothly shaped body and powerfully beating tail, the swordfish can swim at 36 km/h (22 miles per hour).

OCEANIC WHITETIP SHARK

Named for its white-tipped rounded fins, this shark grows to 3 m (9.8 ft) long. It feeds on squid, mahi-mahi, mackerel, and sea turtles, but rarely eats a pilot fish, which it can recognize by its vivid stripes.

PILOT FISH

The pilot fish swims beside sharks, rays, and sea turtles, so it can eat their skin parasites as well as leftover food. It is most often seen with the oceanic whitetip shark. In return for being rid of itchy parasites, the shark gives the pilot fish protection from predators.

PACIFIC SAURY

Like many epipelagic schooling fish, this saury makes long migrations. During its short life, usually lasting no more than four years, the saury travels hundreds of miles every year. It moves between the waters where it feeds and where it lays eggs, due to changing water temperatures and food sources.

MAHI-MAHI

A male mahi-mahi has a large forehead, which helps it attract a female. Both males and females can change the vivid shades of their skin, perhaps to attract mates or to confuse predators. Young mahi-mahi protect themselves by sheltering among floating sargassum seaweed.

Anglerfish

These fish are named for their method of catching prey: Like a human fish-catcher called an angler, they use a "fishing rod" to attract fish. The anglerfish's fishing rod is known as a lure. It is formed from the first spine of the dorsal fin and usually has a fleshy tip.

RED-LIPPED BATFISH

Found around the Pacific Ocean's Galápagos Islands, this fish uses its leg-shaped pectoral, pelvic, and anal fins to walk across the seafloor. Its thick lure makes a smelly chemical that attracts shrimp and worms. The fish's red lips help to attract a mate.

GIGANTIC WHIPNOSE

The whipnose is a deep-sea anglerfish, found at depths of up to 2,500 m (8,200 ft). Its extremely long, glowing lure attracts small fish in the darkness. The fish does not make its own light, but hosts light-making bacteria in the tip of the lure.

SPINYHEAD SEADEVIL

One of the smallest known fish is the male spinyhead seadevil, which reaches 0.7 cm (0.3 in) long. It spends its life attached to a female with its teeth, so it can take nutrients from her blood. The female, which is around 5 cm (2 in) long, has a glowing lure for catching deep-sea fish. When it is time for her to reproduce, the male is helpfully close.

RED HANDFISH

Found only around Australia's Tasmania, this fish is named for its hand-like pectoral fins, on which it walks across the coastal seafloor. It spends much of its time hiding among coral while its lure attracts worms, which mistake the lure's fluffy tip for part of a coral or sponge.

FURRY COFFINFISH

As it rests on the muddy seafloor, this fish's wide, upward-facing mouth can snap up any shrimp attracted by the small lure, which has a moplike tip. When not in use, the lure is lowered into a groove between the eyes. Like a pufferfish, the coffinfish can inflate with water so it is too large for predators to swallow.

Anglerfish Facts

ORDER	Anglerfish
CLADE	Percomorpha
SIZE	0.7–150 cm (0.3–59 in) long
RANGE	All oceans
DIET	Fish and invertebrates

DOUBLE-HOOKED WOLFTRAP ANGLER

This deep-sea anglerfish has movable bones in its upper jaw, which can be folded down to form a toothy cage around the shorter lower jaw, trapping small fish inside. The tip of this wolftrap's lure has two hooks.

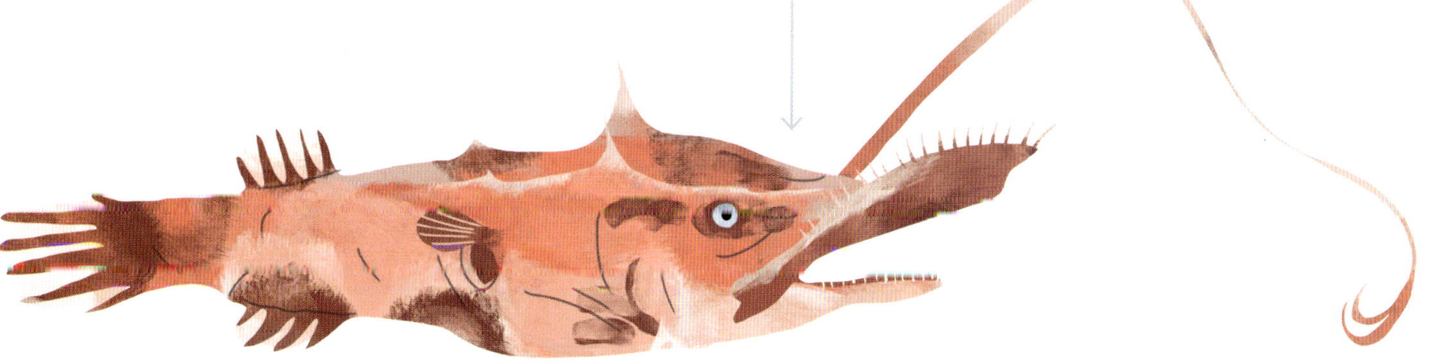

Giant Oarfish

Up to 17 m (56 ft) long, the giant oarfish is the longest of the bony fish, which includes the 28,000 species of fish that do not have skeletons made of cartilage. This oarfish is rarely seen by humans as it usually stays in the mesopelagic zone, also known as the twilight zone. This dimly lit region extends from 200 to 1,000 m (650 to 3,280 ft) below the water surface.

The oarfish swims by rippling its long, ribbon-like body, a bit like a sea snake. Its single dorsal fin extends from its head to the tip of its tail, with the first spines of this fin forming a crest. The fish's pelvic fins are oar-shaped.

STRANGE PROTECTION

The giant oarfish does not have scales for protection, but its skin is coated with guanine. This material is often used in human cosmetics such as lipsticks, where it gives a silvery, pearly sheen. The guanine makes the oarfish's skin reflect what little light reaches into the deep water, making the fish difficult for predators to spot.

In addition, the giant oarfish often hangs almost vertically in the water, with its head uppermost, steadying itself with small movements of its dorsal fin. This helps the oarfish to hide from predators that are on the lookout for the usual, horizontal shape of a fish. The oarfish's narrow, upright body is also difficult to spot from either above or below.

The giant oarfish may have evolved its immense size to protect it from predators. Several oarfish have been seen with their tails missing. This suggests that, unlike most fish, this oarfish can survive severe wounds. Despite its great length, most of the oarfish's organs are concentrated in the front quarter of its body, making the rest of its body little more than a way to distract and frighten away predators.

FISH OF LEGENDS

It is believed that, over the centuries, occasional sightings of the giant oarfish led to sailors telling tales of terrifying "sea serpents." In fact, this fish does not have teeth so is harmless to humans and other large animals. It feeds by taking gulps of water that contains small invertebrates. The food is trapped in the fish's mouth, while the used water flows out through its gills.

Even today, legends surround the giant oarfish. In Japan, some say that these fish wash up on beaches before an earthquake, warning people of what is coming. Scientists wonder if there could be any facts behind this belief. Perhaps the giant oarfish is more easily harmed than other fish by seafloor movements during an offshore earthquake. Their scaleless skin is soft and delicate, while their great length makes them awkward swimmers. These factors might, possibly, make the oarfish more likely to wash up on shore.

Giant Oarfish Facts

SPECIES	*Regalecus glesne*
FAMILY	Oarfish
ORDER	Lampriformes
SIZE	3–17 m (9.8–55.8 ft) long
RANGE	Atlantic, Indian, Pacific, and southern Arctic Oceans
DIET	Zooplankton, small squid, and shrimp

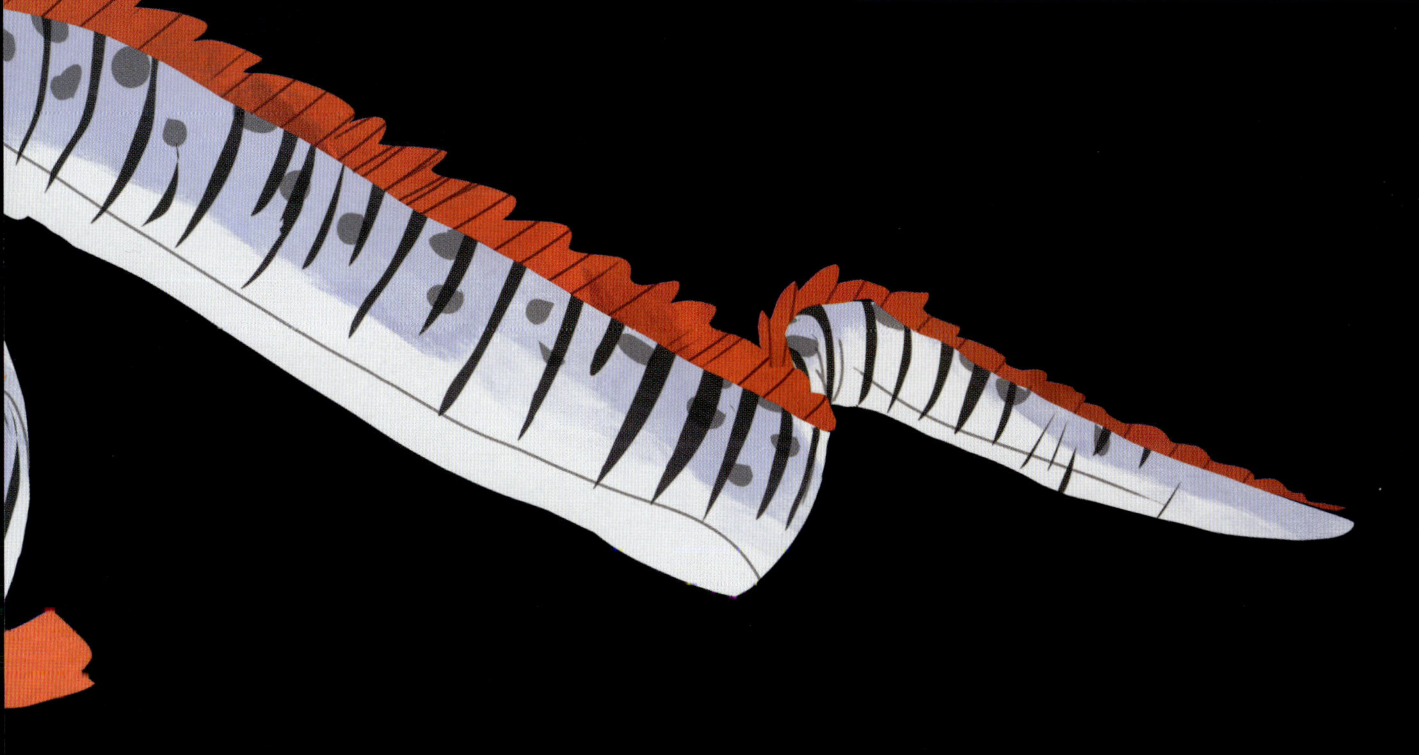

In the Deep Ocean

More than 1,000 m (3,280 ft) below the surface of the Atlantic Ocean, the water is dark both day and night. This region is the bathypelagic zone, also known as the midnight zone. The water here is always cold, ranging from 2 to 4 °C (36 to 39 °F).

Since plants and plantlike algae make their food from sunlight, none can be found in the midnight zone. Without these sources of food, this zone has fewer living things. As a result, many deep-sea fish have very large, wide-opening mouths. This allows them to kill prey that is bigger than themselves, taking advantage of any living thing that can be found.

Many bathypelagic fish have light-making organs called photophores. These make light with a chemical reaction: Two chemicals are mixed together, responding to each other by giving off energy in the form of light. Fish may use light for several purposes: attracting or seeing prey, finding a mate, and camouflaging themselves.

BARRELEYE

This fish swims just below the limit of where sunlight can reach, using its upward-pointing, barrel-shaped eyes to watch the water above for the dark shapes of prey. The fish's eyes have wide lenses, which are protected by the fish's transparent head, allowing it to collect as much sunlight as possible, a little like a telescope.

THREADFIN DRAGONFISH

The dragonfish has a threadlike structure, called a barbel, on its chin. At the barbel's tip are photophores that emit blue-green light. This shade of light travels farthest in the water, helping the fish to attract prey. Photophores on the fish's face emit red light, allowing it to see reddish prey, such as shrimp.

HALF-NAKED HATCHETFISH

Across the hatchetfish's belly are photophores that create a type of camouflage called counter-illumination. The photophores match the amount of light falling from above, so the fish cannot be seen as a dark shape when looking from below.

COMMON FANGTOOTH

With its huge mouth and long teeth, the fangtooth can kill prey larger than itself. When the fish's mouth is closed, the two longest fangs of the lower jaw fit into a pair of sockets in the upper jaw, extending to either side of the brain.

DOFLEINI'S LANTERNFISH

During the day, this fish stays in the relative safety of the deep ocean, but at night it swims toward the surface to feed on zooplankton. Its photophores are arranged in a particular pattern, different for each species of lanternfish, which helps it stay with its shoal and attract a mate.

BLACK SWALLOWER

The black swallower's stomach can stretch to fit prey that is twice the fish's length and ten times its weight. The swallower may seize fish by the tail and then slide itself slowly forward, swallowing the prey until it is coiled inside the stomach.

Mammals

There are around 127 species of marine mammals, ranging in size from the marine otter to the blue whale. Marine mammals belong to different groups that are not closely related to each other. Among them are around 87 species of ocean-living cetaceans, which are commonly called whales, dolphins, and porpoises. Then there are 3 species of ocean-living sirenians, which are often called sea cows. There are also 33 species of marine pinnipeds, a group that includes true seals, fur seals, sea lions, and the walrus. Finally, there is the polar bear and 3 species of otters that spend time in seawater.

Mammals evolved on land around 225 million years ago. The different groups of marine mammals adapted to life in the ocean at different times, starting with cetaceans around 50 million years ago. The different groups adapted to the water to different degrees. All of them must go to the water surface to breathe air into their lungs—but while some whales can stay underwater for up to 222 minutes, the polar bear can last little more than 3 minutes.

Cetaceans and sirenians are fully aquatic, which means they never leave the water. Unlike most mammals, they are nearly hairless. They have flippers for swimming and give birth in the water. Pinnipeds are semiaquatic: They hunt for food in the ocean, but return to land for resting and giving birth. Otters and the polar bear spend much of their time on land, but rely on the ocean for most of their food.

The largest marine mammal is the blue whale, the biggest animal ever known to exist, which reaches 29.9 m (98 ft) long. Despite its immense size, the blue whale eats tiny invertebrates called krill. However, it eats more than 1,000 kg (2,200 lb) of them every day.

The smallest marine mammal is the marine otter, which grows no more than 115 cm (45 in) long, from its nose to the tip of its tail. It is found on rocky shores and in coastal waters of South America. It feeds on whatever animals it can grasp with its claws and sharp teeth, from fish to seabirds.

Baleen Whales

Baleen whales are cetaceans, a group of mammals that never leave water. Cetaceans have streamlined bodies, two flippers, and blowholes on the top of their head, through which they breathe air. Baleen whales do not have teeth: They capture food using comb-like plates.

HUMPBACK WHALE

This whale feeds by taking a big gulp of seawater, expanding grooves along its throat so that it can fit more. Then the whale pushes out the water through bristly plates—made of a tough material called baleen—that hang from its upper jaw. Small animals are caught inside the plates.

PYGMY RIGHT WHALE

The smallest of the baleen whales, the pygmy right still weighs up to 3,500 kg (7,700 lb), more than 38 average adult men. The whale swims in the cool waters of the Southern Ocean, where it is kept warm by thick layers of fat called blubber.

COMMON MINKE WHALE

After a pregnancy lasting 10 months, a female common minke gives birth to one calf. The baby drinks its mother's milk for around 6 months, then swims away. As with most baleen whales, an adult travels alone or in a small group, but will gather in larger numbers in mating or feeding areas.

BRYDE'S WHALE

Bryde's whales sometimes hunt as a group, swimming under and around a group of krill or fish while blowing air from their blowholes. This traps the prey in a "net" of bubbles, allowing the whales to gulp many animals at once.

BOWHEAD WHALE

This whale gets its name for its strong, triangular skull, which it uses to break the ice covering the Arctic Ocean so it can breathe. The bowhead has the world's largest mouth, up to 5 m (16.4 ft) long and 4 m (13 ft) high. It swims along with its mouth open, so that water and small animals—which are trapped by its baleen—flow inside.

NORTH PACIFIC RIGHT WHALE

Like all baleen whales, the North Pacific right uses sound to communicate. Researchers think that different calls, including moans, warbles, and sudden "gunshots," have different meanings. During the mating season, male whales join these calls into songlike patterns.

Baleen Whale Facts

PARVORDER	Baleen whales
INFRAORDER	Cetaceans
SIZE	5–31 m (16.4–101.7 ft) long
RANGE	All oceans
DIET	Small animals, including fish and crustaceans such as krill

In the Kelp Forest

A kelp forest grows in the waters of the Pacific Ocean, off the coast of the US state of California. Although kelps look like plants, they are algae. However, like a plant, kelp attaches itself to the seafloor and uses sunlight to make its own food.

Around 20 species of kelp make up California's kelp forests. The largest species are bull kelp and giant kelp, which can grow to more than 30 m (100 ft) tall. These species thrive in cool and clear water. Air-filled, floating sacs allow the kelp to grow toward the water surface, where there is plenty of sunlight.

Kelp provides food and hiding places for small animals from sea urchins to rockfish. These prey animals attract many marine mammals to the forest. From seals to dolphins, these mammal predators also use the kelp as a hiding place from their own predators, such as orcas.

HARBOR SEAL

This common seal hunts alone for fish such as herring and anchovies in coastal waters. After feeding, it hauls itself ashore to rest, gathering with other seals on sandy beaches or rocky coasts. It spends around half its life on land and half in the water.

SEA OTTER

The sea otter has the thickest fur of any animal, which keeps it warm in the cool waters of the North Pacific Ocean. It sleeps while floating on its back at the water surface. To prevent itself from drifting out to sea, it wraps itself in kelp.

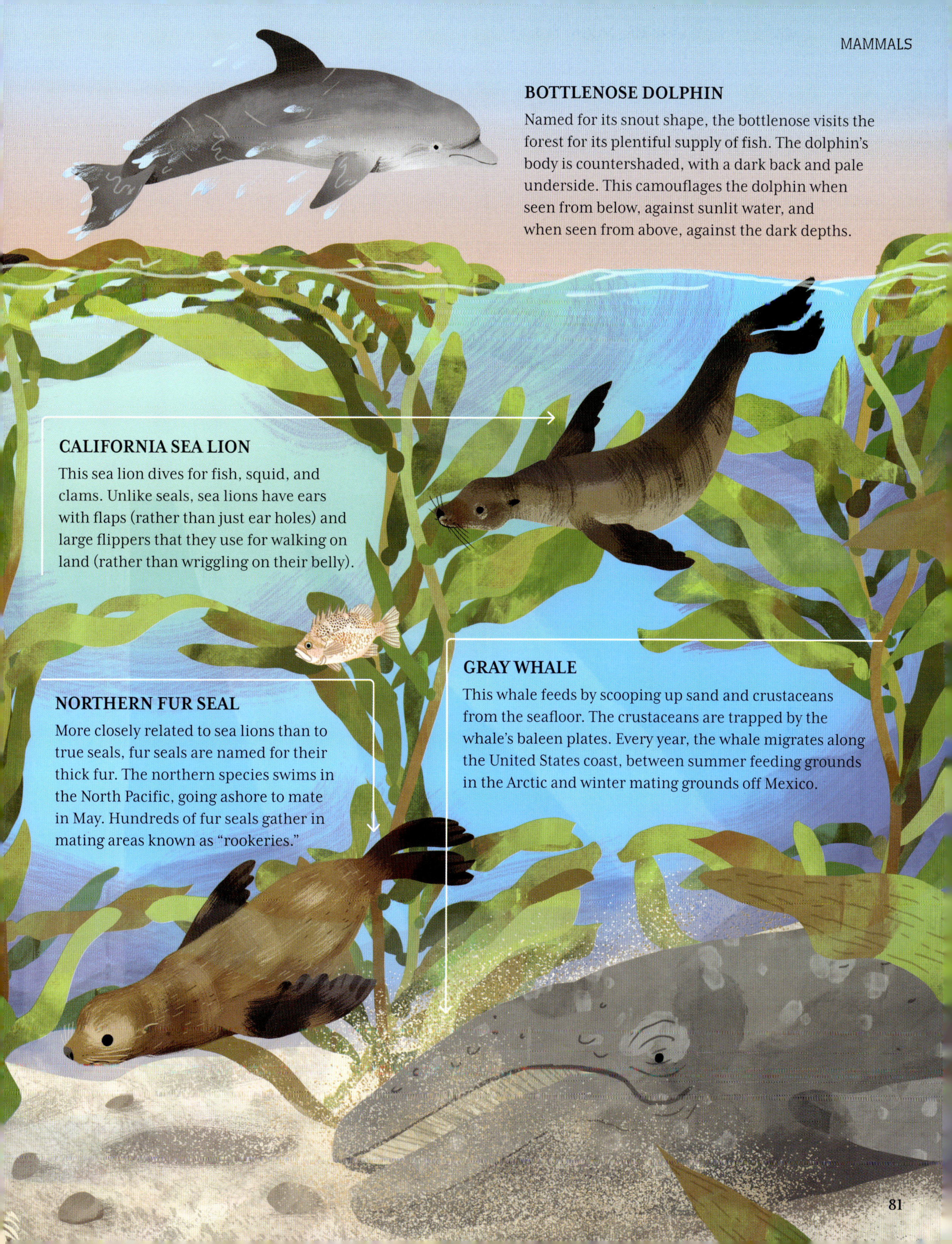

BOTTLENOSE DOLPHIN

Named for its snout shape, the bottlenose visits the forest for its plentiful supply of fish. The dolphin's body is countershaded, with a dark back and pale underside. This camouflages the dolphin when seen from below, against sunlit water, and when seen from above, against the dark depths.

CALIFORNIA SEA LION

This sea lion dives for fish, squid, and clams. Unlike seals, sea lions have ears with flaps (rather than just ear holes) and large flippers that they use for walking on land (rather than wriggling on their belly).

NORTHERN FUR SEAL

More closely related to sea lions than to true seals, fur seals are named for their thick fur. The northern species swims in the North Pacific, going ashore to mate in May. Hundreds of fur seals gather in mating areas known as "rookeries."

GRAY WHALE

This whale feeds by scooping up sand and crustaceans from the seafloor. The crustaceans are trapped by the whale's baleen plates. Every year, the whale migrates along the United States coast, between summer feeding grounds in the Arctic and winter mating grounds off Mexico.

Dugong

This marine mammal eats seagrass, which is a flowering plant that grows in sunlit coastal water. The dugong and its close relatives, the manatees, are the only entirely plant-eating water-living mammals. The dugong can live for up to 70 years, but is endangered due to its near-shore habitat, which puts it at risk from fishing nets, collisions with boats, and pollution.

SEA COWS

The dugong is in the Sirenia scientific order, often known as the "sea cows" because they graze peacefully on seagrass. There are three other species in the order: the Amazonian, West Indian, and West African manatees. Unlike its relatives, the Amazonian manatee lives only in fresh water.

The dugong and manatees look very similar, but can be told apart by their tails. Manatees have paddled-shaped tails, while the dugong has a fluked tail a little like a whale's, which means that it is pointed at the tips and notched in the middle.

Dugong Facts

SPECIES	*Dugong dugon*
ORDER	Sea cows
MIRORDER	Tethytherians
SIZE	2.2–3.4 m (7.2–11 ft) long
RANGE	Warm coastal waters of the Indian and western Pacific Oceans
DIET	Seagrass, plus occasional small invertebrates

ELEPHANT COUSINS

Sea cows are more closely related to elephants than to other marine mammals. Sea cows and elephants are Tethytherians: They share an ancestor that lived 60 million years ago and was a land-living plant-eater. Around 40 million years ago, the ancestor of sea cows waded into shallow water to find plants to eat. From then on, sea cows evolved differently from their land-living cousins: They lost their back legs, their front legs became paddle-like flippers, and their tail flattened so it was suited to beating up and down through the water.

However, like elephants, sea cows have thick, wrinkled skin that is mostly hairless, but does have a few bristle-like hairs. In sea cows, these hairs are sensitive, helping the animal to sense movements in the water.

SUITED TO SEAGRASS

The dugong's body is well suited to grazing on seagrass. Its snout (the projecting nose and mouth) is downturned, which helps it feed on the seafloor. Its large, muscular upper lip is used for digging up whole plants, which are shaken to remove sand then put in a pile, before being eaten. The dugong's peg-like teeth are suited to grinding leaves.

As it feeds, the dugong "walks" on its flippers across the seafloor. It can hold its breath for 6 minutes before surfacing to take in air through its large nostrils. While underwater, valves ("doors" made of body tissue) keep the nostrils closed.

Every few years, a dugong mother gives birth to a single calf in shallow water. The calf is fed on its mother's milk for at least 18 months, but remains with its mother for between 6 and 9 years. Calves stay close to their mother throughout this time, often reaching out to touch her with a flipper.

Toothed Whales

Toothed whales include not only the cetaceans that we call "whales," but also those closely related animals that we call "dolphins" and "porpoises." There are more than 70 species of toothed whales, which usually catch food using their sharp teeth.

BELUGA WHALE

This whale is well suited to its Arctic Ocean habitat: It is white and has no dorsal (back) fin, which helps with camouflage and swimming under sea ice. The bump on its forehead is used for echolocation. The whale makes high calls, which are focused and made louder by the bump's fatty tissue. When those calls bounce off ice and prey, the whale listens for their echoes so it understands its location.

BAIRD'S BEAKED WHALE

Like the rest of the beaked whale family, this whale has a long snout, making it look a little like a dolphin. It has only two pairs of teeth, so it sucks fish and squid into its beak rather than bites. However, males use their teeth for fighting other males over females. Males often have scars from these battles.

DUSKY DOLPHIN

This dolphin can often be seen leaping from the water, spinning, and slapping its tail on the surface. It may leap for fun or to take a look at its surroundings. Like most toothed whales, it travels and hunts in a group called a pod, which numbers from around 6 to 15.

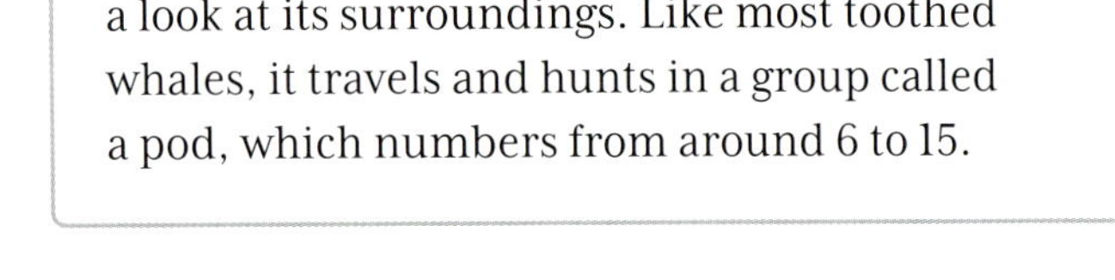

COMMON DOLPHIN

Like other dolphins, this widespread dolphin has a streamlined body suited to swimming at up to 48 km/h (30 miles per hour). It has a beaklike snout with sharp, cone-shaped teeth that can grip slippery, swiftly moving prey, such as fish and squid.

VAQUITA

Just 1.4 m (4.6 ft) long, this porpoise is the smallest cetacean. It is also the most endangered due to its small range, in the Pacific Ocean's Gulf of California, where it is often tangled in nets intended for catching fish.

Toothed Whale Facts

PARVORDER	Toothed whales
INFRAORDER	Cetaceans
SIZE	1.4–20 m (4.6–65.6 ft) long
RANGE	All oceans, as well as some freshwater lakes and rivers
DIET	Fish, squid, crustaceans, seals, and birds

DALL'S PORPOISE

The largest porpoise, this cetacean reaches 2.3 m (7.5 ft) long. Like other members of the porpoise family, it has spade-shaped teeth and no long beak. With small eyes and little sense of smell, it relies on echolocation for hunting fish in dives up to 500 m (1,640 ft) below the surface.

Orca

The orca, also known as the killer whale, is the biggest of all dolphins. Large males can weigh over 10,000 kg (22,000 lb), as much as five family cars. Like other dolphins, the orca is a toothed whale with a streamlined body and strong, cone-shaped teeth. The orca is an apex predator, which means that—when fully grown and healthy—it is too large and powerful to be attacked by other predators.

A LONG LIFE

In the wild, female orcas live up to 80 years, while males usually survive up to 60 years. Orcas live in family groups, which are based around a female, her sons and daughters, and her daughters' children. Due to their long lives, as many as four generations can swim together. For parts of the year, up to four related family groups may swim as a larger group, called a pod.

Adult females always mate with males in a different pod, ensuring that mother and father are not too closely related. After a pregnancy lasting 15 to 18 months, females usually give birth to one calf. Mothers feed their calf on milk for up to 2 years. All adults in the family help to protect their calves.

When swimming close to a coast, orcas often leap from the water—known as "breaching"—to get a better view of their surroundings. They also try to startle and confuse nearby prey by making as loud a sound as possible when they splash back into the water.

LEARNING A LANGUAGE

Like other cetaceans, orcas use sounds to communicate, making clicks, whistles, and buzzes. Within each pod, orcas use the same range of calls, known as a "dialect." Different pods have different "dialects." Just as human babies learn a language from their family, orca calves learn their dialect from listening to their family group.

SMART CETACEANS

Orcas have the second heaviest brain of any animal, with only the sperm whale (see page 35) having a heavier one. An orca brain weighs more than 6 kg (13 lb), much more than the 1.4 kg (3 lb) human brain.

Although intelligence is closely related to how big an animal's brain is compared to its body (which is partly why humans are more intelligent than dolphins), orcas do show signs of intelligence, including playfulness with each other and with boats.

On the coast of Alaska, orcas have learned to steal fish from fisherpeople's hooks. Orcas also "surf" onto beaches in the Indian Ocean's Crozet Islands, using breaking waves to reach resting seals. The orcas wait for the next large wave to pull them back out to sea, along with their prey. Mother orcas shove their calves ashore to learn this trick, waiting close by to help them back into the water if needed.

Orca Facts

SPECIES	*Orcinas orca*
PARVORDER	Toothed whales
INFRAORDER	Cetaceans
SIZE	5–9.8 m (16.4–32 ft) long
RANGE	All oceans
DIET	Seals, dolphins, birds, sea turtles, and fish including sharks

In the Arctic

Throughout the year, the Arctic Ocean keeps a surface temperature of -1.8 °C (28.8 °F), which is near the freezing point of salt water. In winter, when the air temperature at the North Pole falls to -40 °C (-40 °F), more than 14 million sq km (5.4 million sq miles) of the ocean is covered by ice.

Marine mammals that spend all or part of their year in the Arctic Ocean include more than sixteen species of whales, six seals, and two other meat-eaters: the walrus and polar bear. Whales spend all their time in the water, feeding on hardy fish and invertebrates, but come to the surface—finding or making holes in the ice—for air.

Seals and their close relative, the walrus, hunt in the water, but haul themselves onto the ice for mating and resting. The polar bear hunts on the sea ice itself, where its main food is resting seals. In summer, when the sea ice shrinks by half, the polar bear swims ashore, where it survives on a poor diet of Arctic foxes, berries, and kelp.

BEARDED SEAL

Bearded seals are named for their thick, sensitive whiskers, which they use as feelers while they search for clams, crabs, sea cucumbers, and worms in the seafloor mud. Both underwater and on the ice, these seals call to each other using long trills and lower moans.

NARWHAL

A toothed whale, the narwhal lives mostly in the Arctic Ocean, where it is preyed on by polar bears and orcas. The male has a tusk up to 3 m (9.8 ft) long, which grows in a spiral from the upper left side of its jaw. The tusk is an extra-long tooth. Males show off their tusk to attract females.

HARP SEAL

This seal is kept warm by a layer of fat, called blubber, up to 6 cm (2.4 in) thick. It can hold its breath for around 20 minutes as it dives for fish such as polar cod and invertebrates such as krill.

WALRUS

An adult male walrus can weigh 2,000 kg (4,400 lb) and have tusks—which are upper front teeth—up to 1 m (3.3 ft) long. A walrus uses its tusks for making breathing holes in the ice and for dragging itself out of the water onto the slippery ice.

POLAR BEAR

The largest species of bear, the polar bear grows up to 3 m (9.8 ft) long. It spends most of its life on the ice, where it is camouflaged by its white fur. The bear's most common prey is harp, bearded, and ringed seals. It sometimes catches narwhals when they breathe at ice holes. The bear can swim at up to 10 km/h (6 miles per hour) between ice floes.

RINGED SEAL

A female ringed seal makes a cave in the snow on top of the ice, where she gives birth to a single pup in spring. Pups are fed on milk for the first month, while they build up a thick layer of blubber. Young pups have white fur, so they are well camouflaged on the ice, but develop a dark coat with pale rings.

Reptiles

There are around 12,000 species of reptiles, but only around 100 of them spend some or all of their lives in the ocean. Marine reptiles belong to four groups: turtles, crocodiles, snakes, and lizards. There are seven ocean-living turtles, two crocodiles, and just one lizard: the marine iguana. All the other marine reptiles are sea snakes.

The first reptiles evolved around 312 million years ago. They lived on land, laid eggs on land, and had lungs for breathing air. However, around 299 million years ago, some reptiles started to adapt to life in the ocean. While the turtles, crocodiles, and marine iguana evolved the ability to swim, they still lay eggs on land. They must go regularly to the water surface to breathe air into their lungs. Sea snakes are the most adapted to ocean life. Most of them never return to land, instead giving birth to live babies in the water. Although sea snakes do swim to the surface to breathe air, most also have skin that soaks up oxygen from the water, allowing them to stay underwater for up to 8 hours.

All reptiles have thin skin that is protected by scales or scutes. These contain keratin, a tough material also found in hair, nails, and feathers. Scales are usually small and plate-like, while scutes are thicker and bonier. Lizards and snakes have small, overlapping scales. Crocodiles and turtles have scutes on exposed areas, such as a crocodile's back and a turtle's shell.

Green sea turtles lay eggs on a beach. After hatching, baby turtles run to the sea as quickly as possible to avoid predators such as crabs and gulls.

The marine iguana lives on beaches in the Pacific Ocean's Galápagos Islands. It can dive for up to an hour while it feeds on algae on the seabed. Since reptiles cannot make their own body heat, it warms up after swimming by lying in the sunshine.

Sea Turtles

From largest to smallest, the seven species of sea turtles are the leatherback, green (shown on page 96), loggerhead, flatback, hawksbill, olive ridley, and Kemp's ridley. Sea turtles are shelled reptiles that swim by paddling their four flippers.

LOGGERHEAD SEA TURTLE

Loggerheads can live for more than 60 years. Like all sea turtles, loggerheads spend their whole life in the ocean, with only the females coming ashore briefly to lay eggs. These are laid in a hole dug on a beach, then covered by sand. Females nest on or near the beach where they were born.

HAWKSBILL SEA TURTLE

The hawksbill has a sharp, jagged-edged, curving beak, a little like the beak of a hawk. This beak shape allows the turtle to reach into holes and crevices in coral reefs, then tear apart its preferred prey: sponges.

FLATBACK SEA TURTLE

Like other sea turtles, the flatback has a bony shell to protect its organs. Like all sea turtles except the leatherback, the flatback's shell is covered by large scales called scutes. The shell's upper portion is called the carapace, while the section that covers the turtle's underside is the plastron. The flatback's carapace is flatter than those of other sea turtles.

OLIVE RIDLEY SEA TURTLE

This turtle is named for the olive-green shade of its carapace. Thousands of female olive ridleys can nest on the same beach at once. On the coast of the Indian state of Odisha, over 600,000 have been known to nest in one week.

KEMP'S RIDLEY SEA TURTLE

This is the most endangered sea turtle, due to pollution and disturbance on the beaches—in the Atlantic Ocean's Gulf of Mexico—where females lay eggs. Around 100 eggs are laid in each nest. If the nest's temperature is below 29.5 °C (85 °F), the hatchlings will be mainly male; if it is hotter, they will be female.

LEATHERBACK SEA TURTLE

The leatherback has larger flippers and lungs than other sea turtles. As a result, it can dive deeper—down to 1,200 m (4,000 ft)—and stay underwater for longer, up to 85 minutes. Unlike the shells of other sea turtles, the leatherback's is covered only by leathery skin.

Sea Turtle Facts

SUPERFAMILY	Sea turtles
ORDER	Turtles
SIZE	0.6–1.8 m (2–6 ft) long
RANGE	Atlantic, Indian, and Pacific Oceans
DIET	Algae, seagrass, and animals including fish, jellyfish, crabs, and worms

American Crocodile

A little smaller than the saltwater crocodile, the American crocodile is the second largest reptile that commonly swims in the ocean. It weighs up to 900 kg (2,000 lb), more than 10 adult men. Although this crocodile is dangerous to humans due to its immense size and sharp teeth, it is shyer and less aggressive than some of its relatives.

SALT LOVER

This crocodile is found from the southern United States to northern South America, where it lives on beaches and islands, in coastal waters, and even far offshore in the Caribbean Sea. Although the crocodile is sometimes seen in rivers, it seems to prefer salt water.

Most land and freshwater reptiles cannot survive for long in salt water, since drinking salt water or soaking up salt through their skin would damage their organs. However, the American crocodile has salt glands in its tongue. Salt in the crocodile's blood is collected by the glands, then expelled through the nostrils.

American Crocodile Facts

SPECIES	*Crocodylus acutus*
FAMILY	Crocodiles
ORDER	Crocodilians
SIZE	2.9–6.1 m (9.5–20 ft) long
RANGE	Warm coasts and shallow seas of the western Atlantic and eastern Pacific Oceans
DIET	Crabs, turtles, snakes, birds, and small mammals

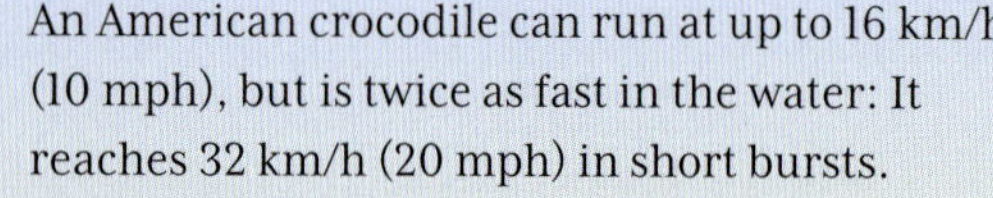

An American crocodile can run at up to 16 km/h (10 mph), but is twice as fast in the water: It reaches 32 km/h (20 mph) in short bursts.

CROCODILE CHARACTER

The American crocodile is a member of the crocodilian order, which includes crocodiles, alligators, caimans, and gharials. Like other crocodiles, the American has a streamlined body: It is smoothly shaped, so it can slide easily through the water. It swims by waving its long, powerful tail. It steers and wades with its webbed feet, which have skin between the toes to make them paddle-like.

The crocodile's snout is long, narrow, and able to open wide to grasp large prey such as turtles, flamingos, and young crocodilians. Its jaws are closed by strong muscles, giving it a deadly bite. It has around 68 cone-shaped teeth.

EGG CARE

American crocodiles mate in early winter. Male crocodiles make low, loud, bellowing noises to attract a female. After mating, the female makes a large mound of sand, mud, and leaves at the water's edge. When she is ready, she makes a hole in the nest and lays 30 to 70 eggs inside. Each whitish egg is around 8 cm (3 in) long and takes up to 80 days to hatch. During that time, both the father and mother guard the nest, attacking predators—such as foxes and vultures—fiercely.

Around 25 cm (10 in) long at birth, baby crocodiles can hunt for insects and small fish within a few days. However, their mother stays close to them for the first five weeks, responding to her babies' calls and watching for predators.

In the Seagrass

Many marine reptiles can be found in a seagrass meadow off the coast of Indonesia. In these warm, shallow waters of the western Pacific Ocean, there is enough sunlight for these plants to make their own food. The seagrass provides food and shelter for prey and predators.

Most marine reptiles—apart from some sea turtles, which swim into deeper water—live in warm coastal waters, not far from the equator. Since reptiles cannot control their own body temperature, they are usually only as warm as the surrounding water: Most marine reptiles need to stay in warm water to survive.

Some marine reptiles, including the saltwater crocodile and sea kraits, stay close to land so they can go ashore to lay eggs, rest, and bask in the sunshine to warm up. However, like most sea snakes, the yellow-bellied and ornate sea snakes spend their whole lives in the water. The meadow offers them shelter and easy prey: Countless fish lay their eggs among the seagrass, filling the meadow with young fish.

YELLOW-BELLIED SEA SNAKE

Like other sea snakes, this snake's body is adapted for swimming: It is flattened from side to side and its tail is paddle-like. By making sideways wriggling motions, the snake can swim at up to 3.6 km/h (2.2 miles per hour).

GREEN SEA TURTLE

This turtle is named for the green fat under its carapace. The fat gets this hue from the turtle's diet of green seagrass and seaweed. The turtle must swim to the surface to breathe, but it can sleep underwater—with its body processes slowed—for several hours, by wedging itself under a ledge in rocks or corals.

SALTWATER CROCODILE

The world's largest reptile, this crocodile grows to 6.3 m (20.7 ft) long. It preys on any animal that enters its territory, from turtles and snakes to water buffalo. The crocodile ambushes prey by swimming slowly underwater toward it, then leaping suddenly upward—giving the strongest bite of any animal.

YELLOW-LIPPED SEA KRAIT

This snake spends half of its life on land, where it rests, mates, and lays eggs in caves and rock crevices. Since the sea krait's flattened body is shaped for swimming, it moves more slowly on land: Its crawling speed is around one-fifth of its swimming speed.

ORNATE SEA SNAKE

Like nearly all sea snakes, this snake is venomous. The snake's bold pattern is a warning to predators of this fact. The ornate sea snake injects prey—such as small fish—with venom using its sharp, hollow fangs, which are connected to venom-making glands.

BLUE-LIPPED SEA KRAIT

This sea snake lives in the warm, shallow waters of the Indian and western Pacific Oceans. It uses its powerful sense of smell to find prey such as eels and other small fish. Its venom is strong enough to be deadly to humans, but this shy snake only bites humans to defend itself.

Birds

Out of 10,000 species of birds, more than 350 depend on the oceans for food. The birds commonly called seabirds are those that take all or most of their food from the ocean. Seabirds are in these scientific orders: Sphenisciformes (penguins), Procellariiformes (albatrosses and petrels), Suliformes (boobies, cormorants, frigatebirds, and gannets), and Charadriiformes (auks, gulls, skimmers, skuas, and terns). Some other birds—including sea eagles, sea ducks, pelicans, and wading shorebirds—take some of their food from the coastal ocean.

Different bird groups have developed different strategies and body shapes for hunting in, on, and around the ocean. Some, such as auks and penguins, have flipper-like wings for swimming beneath the water surface. Others, such as albatrosses and frigatebirds, have wide wings for soaring over the vast ocean as they watch for swimming prey—which they pluck from the surface. Wading birds have long legs for feeding in the shallows, while sea ducks have broad bodies suited to swimming at the ocean surface.

Many of these ocean-feeding birds share some similarities. Most have webbed feet, with skin and tissue joining the toes, which is helpful for paddling in water or walking on soft shores without sinking. Many ocean-feeding birds have salt glands, which are organs that draw out salt from the blood then expel it through the beak. Without such glands, seabirds would die from excess salt taken in while drinking and feeding. Due to their stormy, changeable habitat, most seabirds lay fewer eggs than land birds, so they can give extra-careful attention to each chick.

The macaroni penguin is a seabird in the Sphenisciformes order. It dives up to 100 m (330 ft) beneath the surface of the Southern Ocean in search of krill, squid, and fish.

To attract a female, a male blue-footed booby shows off his feet by lifting them up and down. Females choose mates with brighter feet, which is a sign of youth and health. A bright-footed male is therefore a good choice for breeding and parenting.

Auks

The auks are a family of 23 seabirds that spend most of their life in, on, or above the open sea. Although auks can fly, their small, flipper-like wings are better suited to powering the bird underwater as they chase prey.

ATLANTIC PUFFIN

This puffin comes ashore only to mate and nest, which it does with the same partner throughout its life. The female lays a single white egg in a hole dug on a clifftop. Puffins nest in huge groups, called colonies, with up to a million or more birds.

TUFTED PUFFIN

Like other auks, this puffin has an upright stance when on land. It hunts by paddling at the ocean surface, then diving up to 60 m (200 ft) deep for squid, krill, and small fish. Its wings are too short for gliding (soaring without flapping), but it can fly by fluttering fast, after making a running start to get into the air.

CRESTED AUKLET

Both male and female crested auklets have evolved features that catch the attention of a mate: a forehead crest, a smell like lemons, and a trumpeting call. Birds with bigger crests and a stronger smell usually find a mate sooner. The loud calls help to keep that bond.

SPECTACLED GUILLEMOT

This auk is named for the white patches around its eyes, which look a little like spectacles. It nests on rocky coasts of northeastern Asia, where the female lays two eggs in a crevice each year. The chicks are fed by their parents for 6 weeks, until they are able to fly.

RAZORBILL

The razorbill uses its thick, sharp-edged beak for capturing fish such as herring and hake. Chicks leave their cliff nest at just 20 days old, before they have grown feathers strong enough for flight. The chicks jump into the water, where they are fed by their father until they can hunt.

DOVEKIE

Also known as the little auk, this is one of the smallest auks. In spring and summer, it nests on Arctic Ocean islands, but it moves south to the North Atlantic Ocean in winter. Its main predators are Arctic foxes and the glaucous seagull.

Auk Facts

FAMILY	Auks
ORDER	Charadriiformes
SIZE	15–45 cm (6–18 in) long
RANGE	Coasts and open water of the North Atlantic and North Pacific Oceans
DIET	Fish and invertebrates such as krill and squid

White-Tailed Eagle

This powerful bird seizes most of its food from the coastal ocean or from freshwater lakes and rivers. It is a bird of prey, which means it feeds on other vertebrates using its sharp beak and claws. With a wingspan—from wingtip to wingtip—of up to 2.4 m (8 ft), the white-tailed eagle is one of the largest birds of prey.

SEA EAGLE

The white-tailed eagle is a sea eagle, a group of eagles that usually make ocean fish a large part of their diet. Like most eagles, the white-tailed has a big head and huge beak. The beak is strong and hooked, making it suitable for ripping flesh, while the eagle's toes end in long claws called talons.

Like other eagles, the white-tailed has extremely good eyesight, allowing it to see around twice as far as a human. This is partly due to its extra-large pupils, which are the holes that allow light to enter the eye. As the eagle flies high over the ocean, it can see fish just below the water surface.

HUNTING AND STEALING

When hunting over the ocean, the eagle watches for fish and floating water birds such as ducks, then swoops to the surface. It grasps prey with its talons, usually getting only its feet wet. Sometimes, however, it plunges beneath the water to snatch fish. At other times, the eagle wades into shallow water from a beach.

This eagle also steals food. It follows fishing boats so it can take their catch from the deck. In addition, it snatches food from sea otters, cormorants, and gulls.

White-Tailed Eagle Facts

SPECIES	*Haliaeetus albicilla*
SUBFAMILY	Sea eagles
ORDER	Accipitriformes
SIZE	66–94 cm (26–37 in) long
RANGE	Coasts and inland fresh water of Europe and Asia
DIET	Fish, water birds, and small mammals, such as squirrels

A PAIR FOR LIFE

White-tailed eagles stay with the same mate for life, after first finding a partner when they are 5 or 6 years old. The pair builds a nest from twigs on a cliff or in a tall tree close to the coast or inland water. The nest is huge, around 1 m (3.3 ft) across and 2 m (6.6 ft) deep. It is lined with seaweed or plants. The female lays one or two eggs each spring. Until chicks can fly, after around 70 days of life, they are brought food by both parents.

Usually, the mating pair stays in the nest area throughout their lives, which may be around 20 years. The pair will roost—sleeping and resting—together. Sometimes, they hunt together, with one creating confusion among a flock of birds, while the other goes in for the kill.

This eagle prefers to catch fish that are 30 to 60 cm (12 to 24 in) long. Smaller fish are less worth the effort, while larger fish may be too heavy to carry. After catching prey, the bird flies to a high perch before eating.

On a Rocky Shore

The tiny Canadian island of Ile Bonaventure lies 5 km (3 miles) off the mainland, at the edge of the northwestern Atlantic Ocean. With no human homes or industry, the island is an important bird sanctuary, visited—or lived on year-round—by 218 species.

During the breeding season, which runs from April to October depending on the species, the island's cliffs, beaches, and forests are home to large colonies of nesting birds. In these months, the island's 4 sq km (1.5 sq miles) can host 280,000 birds.

Birds have different strategies to keep their nest safe from predators. Many seabirds nest on cliff ledges that land predators—such as red foxes—cannot reach, while the great number of birds in a nesting colony gives protection from winged attackers such as gulls. Shyer birds hide their nests among rocks or plants. Only more aggressive birds, such as the great black-backed gull, nest on more open ground.

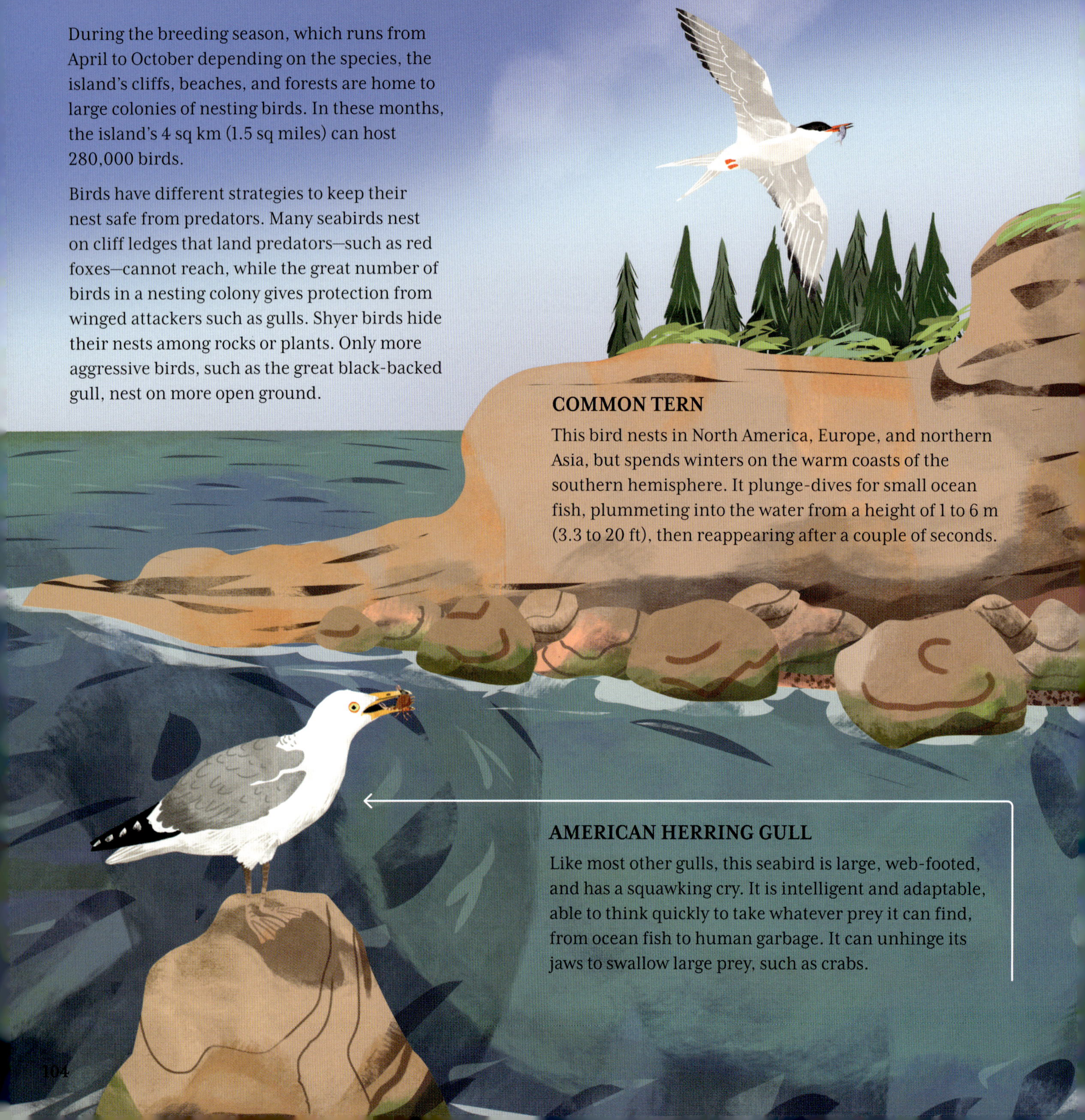

COMMON TERN

This bird nests in North America, Europe, and northern Asia, but spends winters on the warm coasts of the southern hemisphere. It plunge-dives for small ocean fish, plummeting into the water from a height of 1 to 6 m (3.3 to 20 ft), then reappearing after a couple of seconds.

AMERICAN HERRING GULL

Like most other gulls, this seabird is large, web-footed, and has a squawking cry. It is intelligent and adaptable, able to think quickly to take whatever prey it can find, from ocean fish to human garbage. It can unhinge its jaws to swallow large prey, such as crabs.

NORTHERN GANNET

The largest seabird in the northern Atlantic Ocean, this gannet has a wingspan of up to 1.8 m (5.9 ft). As many as 60,000 pairs nest on the cliffs of Ile Bonaventure, where the surrounding water is cool enough for the Atlantic mackerel and herring that the gannet eats.

BLACK-LEGGED KITTIWAKE

A member of the gull family, this bird gets its English name from its high-pitched call: "kittee-wa-aaake, kitte-wa-aaake." From May to September, it nests on steep cliffs. It spends the rest of the year at sea, watching for surface-swimming fish while flying over, or floating on, the water surface.

LEACH'S STORM PETREL

Just 21 cm (8 in) long, this small seabird nests in a rocky crevice, coming out only at night, so it can stay hidden from fierce gulls. Outside the breeding season, it comes to land only during the fiercest storms.

GREAT BLACK-BACKED GULL

The largest gull, this seabird weighs up to 2.3 kg (5 lb). In spring, it nests in a hollow—lined with grass, twigs, seaweed, or moss—on top of stones or a log. Both parents defend the nest, then take turns feeding the chicks for their first 6 months.

Brown Pelican

The brown pelican feeds by plunge-diving—beak first—into the coastal ocean, from a height of 18 to 21 m (60 to 70 ft) above the water surface. When the bird hits the water, it may be moving at 64 km/h (40 miles per hour). The pelican aims for shoals of small fish, which it spies as it cruises above the ocean.

FALLING WELL

As human divers know, hitting water from a great height can be painful and dangerous. A key to avoiding injury is to hit the water surface with as little of the body as possible. To understand why, slap bathwater with an open palm, then slice it with the side of your hand.

Although a brown pelican starts dives with its wings open, it folds them back before reaching the water. In addition, the bird inflates air sacs in its neck and belly, which cushion the blow and protect its organs.

CATCHING FISH

After the pelican hits the water, it opens its long beak and inflates a flap in its throat, known as a gular pouch. The bird traps small fish—as well as water—inside its mouth and pouch. Then the pelican swims back to the water surface within no more than a few seconds.

While resting on the water surface, the pelican opens its beak to drain out the water before swallowing its fish. Occasionally, fierce birds—such as laughing gulls—steal fish out of the pelican's mouth as it drains.

STAYING WITH A FLOCK

Unlike many seabirds, which live alone except during the breeding season, the brown pelican spends all its life in a flock. In spring, the flock forms mating pairs, making new partnerships each year. Both males and females perform mating displays to attract a partner, including bowing, swaying, and making loud calls.

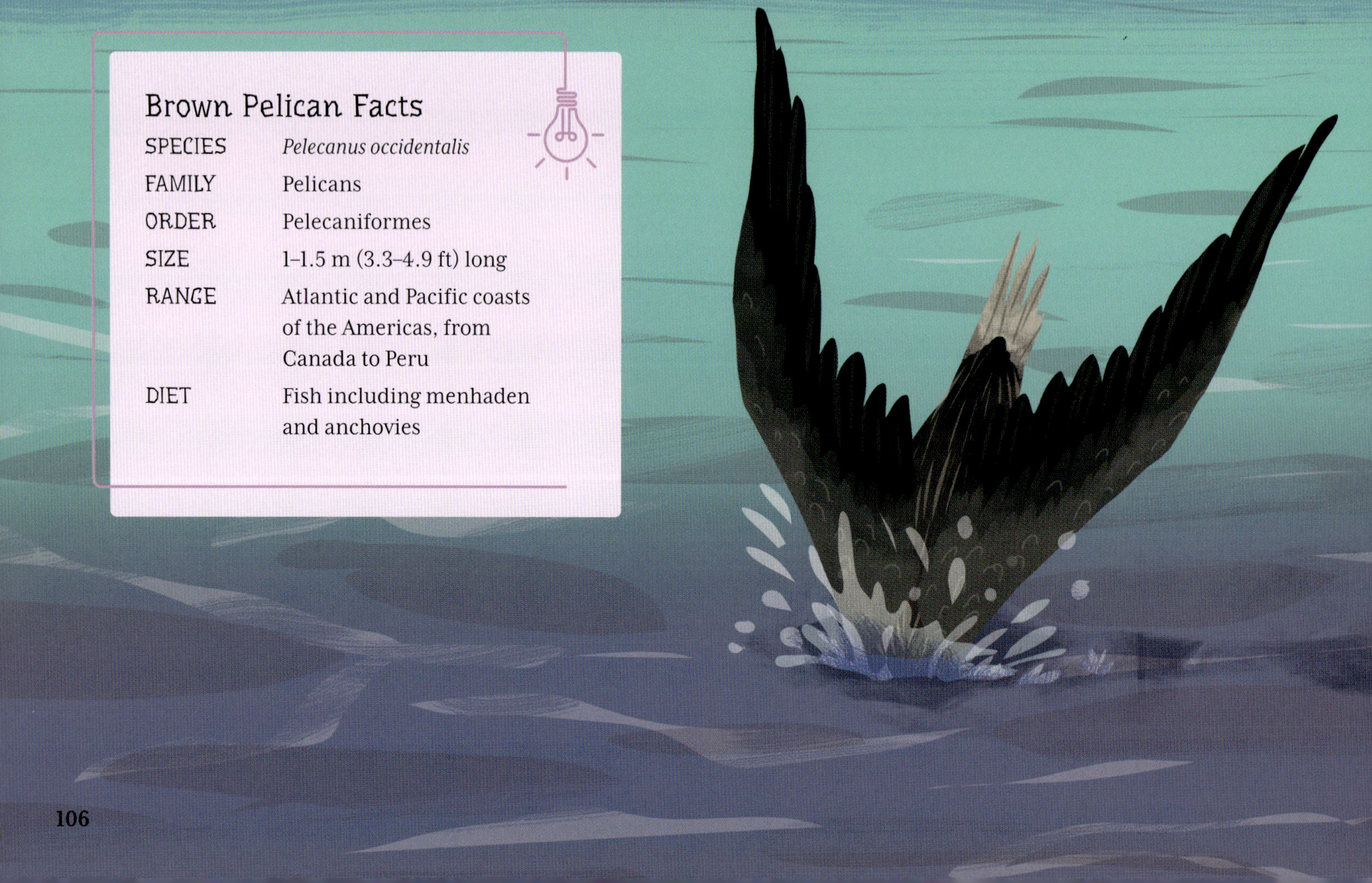

Brown Pelican Facts

SPECIES	*Pelecanus occidentalis*
FAMILY	Pelicans
ORDER	Pelecaniformes
SIZE	1–1.5 m (3.3–4.9 ft) long
RANGE	Atlantic and Pacific coasts of the Americas, from Canada to Peru
DIET	Fish including menhaden and anchovies

Before laying two or three eggs, the female builds a nest of sticks, reeds, and leaves, either on the ground among shrubs or in coastal trees, such as mangroves. Until the eggs hatch, both parents take turns warming them. Even though chicks can fly by the age of 3 months, they are fed by their parents for up to 10 months. The parents spit up partly digested fish for them.

As a brown pelican dives, it rotates a little to the left, so that it does not injure its windpipe, which runs along the right side of its neck.

Cormorants

These dark-feathered birds catch fish in their beak by diving from the ocean surface, pushing themselves through the water with their wide, webbed feet. After diving, cormorants go ashore to spread their wings to dry in the sunshine, since their feathers are not fully waterproof.

FLIGHTLESS CORMORANT

Found on the Pacific Ocean's Galápagos Islands, where there are few land-living predators, this is the only cormorant that has lost the ability to fly. Over millions of years, its wings became better and better suited to swimming—and too short to lift a bird of this size into the air.

DOUBLE-CRESTED CORMORANT

This bird is named for the two crests it grows during the breeding season. Both the male and female help to build a stick nest in a tree, on a cliff, or on the ground on an isolated island. The female lays two to four eggs, which are warmed by both parents for a month before hatching.

RED-LEGGED CORMORANT

Unlike most cormorants, this bird does not nest in a colony, but in a pair or a small group. When choosing a mate, males and females perform a mating display, with hopping, chirping, and neck-stretching. Nests are built on cliffs from poop, feathers, and seaweed.

RED-FACED CORMORANT

During the breeding season, adult red-faced cormorants grow two head crests, while the bare red skin on their face becomes brighter. While young birds are not mature enough to mate, they often "play" at mating during the season, building an eggless nest at the edge of the colony's cliff.

BRANDT'S CORMORANT

This cormorant dives for herring and rockfish in the coastal waters of the western United States. It swims as deep as 70 m (230 ft), holding its breath for up to 3 minutes, while making long, powerful strokes with both feet at once.

GREAT CORMORANT

This common bird eats bottom-dwelling fish such as sculpin and flounder, using its long, hooked beak to pull them out from rock crevices. The cormorant swallows small fish while underwater, but brings larger prey to the surface to kill it first with shaking and biting.

Cormorant Facts

FAMILY	Cormorants and shags
ORDER	Suliformes
SIZE	45–100 cm (18–39 in) long
RANGE	Coasts and coastal waters of all oceans, as well as inland fresh water
DIET	Fish, invertebrates, and water snakes

Greater Flamingo

This tall bird is the largest of the six species of flamingos. It lives in a large, noisy colony in shallow coastal water or on mudflats, where it feeds on tiny living things. Like other flamingos, it is not born pink, but turns pink because of the food it eats.

FILLTER-FEEDING

The greater flamingo eats tiny invertebrates such as brine shrimp and insects, as well as minuscule cyanobacteria. It filters these living things from water and mud using its beak, which has hairy, comb-like structures along its inside edges. The flamingo bends down, using its long, flexible neck to reach the muddy bottom with its head upside down.

The flamingo opens its hooked beak—which is almost bowl-shaped when upside down—and sucks in water. Then it lets the water drain away, using its large, rough-surfaced tongue to help the process, leaving food trapped in the beak.

TURNING PINK

Shrimp and cyanobacteria contain pink pigments (chemicals that create color) called carotenoids, which are also in carrots and tomatoes. By the time a flamingo is two years old, its feathers are pink due to the quantity of pigments it has eaten. Humans would see a similar effect in their own skin if they ate lots of carrots every day for several months.

MATING DANCES

Greater flamingos often keep the same mate for life. At the start of the yearly mating season, the colony performs dances, which may help young birds to find a mate for the first time, while also strengthening the bond between existing couples. Both males and females dance: They stretch their neck, turn their head, and flap their wings.

Birds also make themselves pinker for the mating season, by spreading extra pigment-containing oil from their preen gland, which is at the base of the tail. Most birds have a preen gland, which makes oil that is spread through feathers using the beak, keeping them flexible and waterproof.

Each female flamingo lays one large egg, up to 9 cm (3.5 in) long, on a mound of mud, which keeps the egg above water level. Once a brownish, fluffy chick has hatched, it is fed by both parents: They make red "crop milk" in glands in their throat, then spit it into the chick's mouth. From two weeks old, the colony's chicks move into adult-free groups, known as crèches, which contain thousands of young birds that stick together for safety.

Greater Flamingo Facts

SPECIES	*Phoenicopterus roseus*
FAMILY	Flamingos
ORDER	Phoenicopteriformes
SIZE	1.1–1.8 m (3.6–5.9 ft) tall
RANGE	Coasts of Africa, southern Europe, and southern Asia
DIET	Small invertebrates, algae, bacteria, and seeds

The greater flamingo's long legs allow it to wade through shallow water while keeping its feathers dry. The joint at the middle of the flamingo's leg is its ankle, not its knee, so it appears that its legs bend backward as it walks. The bird has wide, webbed feet, which spread its weight so that it does not sink into the mud. The feet are also used to stir up mud, freeing tiny creatures to eat.

On a Salt Marsh

Wading birds, kingfishers, and even songbirds can be spotted in a Mexican salt marsh. These coastal marshes are found on low-lying land that is regularly flooded with salt water by the tides. Across the world, at least 90,000 sq km (35,000 sq miles) is salt marsh.

A salt marsh is home to plants that can live in salt water. This makes them different from 98 percent of plants. These salt-tolerant plants include grasses, sedges, and glasswort. Some of them have evolved to have salt glands, which release the harmful salts that are soaked up through their roots.

This is a busy habitat, visited by animal species from both ocean and land, as well as those—such as wading birds—that have evolved to live where water meets land. Flounder and other sea fish, as well as ocean invertebrates such as shrimp, lay eggs and spend their youth in the shelter of the marsh. Crabs burrow in the mud, while caterpillars crawl on the plants. Drawn by the plentiful food, dozens of bird species are residents or visitors.

BELTED KINGFISHER

The belted kingfisher plunges into water headfirst to catch small fish in its sharp beak. It breeds in Canada and Alaska, but flies south to spend the winter in Mexico or the Caribbean.

ROSEATE SPOONBILL

Like a flamingo, this spoonbill gets its pink feathers from a diet of pigment-containing invertebrates. It feeds by swinging its beak through shallow water, using the spoonlike tip to stir up the mud.

WHITE IBIS

The white ibis uses its long beak to probe in shallow water for slow-moving crustaceans such as crabs. It hunts by feel, not by sight, which means that quicker prey—such as darting fish—can escape the bird's snapping beak.

MARSH WREN

The wren is not a seabird or wading shorebird, but a songbird: a common group of land birds with complex calls. It hunts for insects and spiders among the marsh plants. In the breeding season, the male weaves several nests from reeds, so that he can attract a female with his skill.

GREAT BLUE HERON

This large wader finds prey by sight: It watches shallow water for fish, which it spears with its sharp beak. It uses several hunting methods: standing still, walking slowly, swimming, and hovering over the water.

BLACK SKIMMER

This fish-eating bird is found in large colonies in coastal habitats from salt marshes and mudflats to beaches and bays. It feeds by skimming the water surface, flying low with its beak open. The beak has a larger bottom jaw, which helps with scooping.

Sea Ducks

While most ducks live in and near fresh water, around 20 species are often found in the coastal ocean. Ducks have webbed feet and broad bodies suited to floating at the water surface. Their beaks have different shapes for catching their particular prey.

SPECTACLED EIDER

As in most duck species, the male spectacled eider (known as a drake) has brighter plumage than the female (known as a hen). However, outside the breeding season, the drake loses his mate-attracting feathers, turning brown like the female.

HARLEQUIN DUCK

This duck gets its name from the bright plumage of mating males, which looks like the patterned costume of an early Italian drama character named Arlecchino. The duck feeds by diving from the water surface for snails, clams, and crabs.

LONG-TAILED DUCK

In summer, this duck nests on marshes and near lakes in the Arctic regions of North America, Europe, and Asia. It spends the winter on the coastal ocean, often in a large flock. It can dive 60 m (200 ft) deep to pluck hard-shelled clams and cockles with its broad, short beak.

HOODED MERGANSER

This duck's long, thin, jagged-edged beak is ideal for grasping small slippery fish. It mates and nests around lakes and streams in North America, but in winter it may be spotted in sheltered ocean bays.

BUFFLEHEAD

The bufflehead nests in tree-trunk holes close to water. These holes were usually made by a woodpecker for its own nest, then abandoned. A female bufflehead lays around nine eggs in the same hole every year.

WHITE-WINGED SCOTER

The large, broad beak of this duck is suited to grasping tough-shelled clams. Like all birds, the duck has no teeth, but it does have a second, extra-muscly stomach called a gizzard. The scoter's huge gizzard is able to squeeze and crack the shells together until they are crushed.

Sea Duck Facts

TRIBE	Sea ducks
ORDER	Anseriformes
SIZE	32–71 cm (13–28 in) long
RANGE	Coasts and coastal waters of the North Atlantic, North Pacific, and Arctic Oceans, as well as inland fresh water
DIET	Fish, invertebrates such as shellfish, and water plants

Snowy Albatross

Also known as the wandering albatross, this huge seabird has the widest wingspan of any living bird, reaching 3.7 m (12 ft) from wingtip to wingtip. Such long wings allow this albatross to be the bird that probably flies the farthest, covering up to 120,000 km (75,000 miles) in a year as it glides over the southern oceans, circling the globe up to three times.

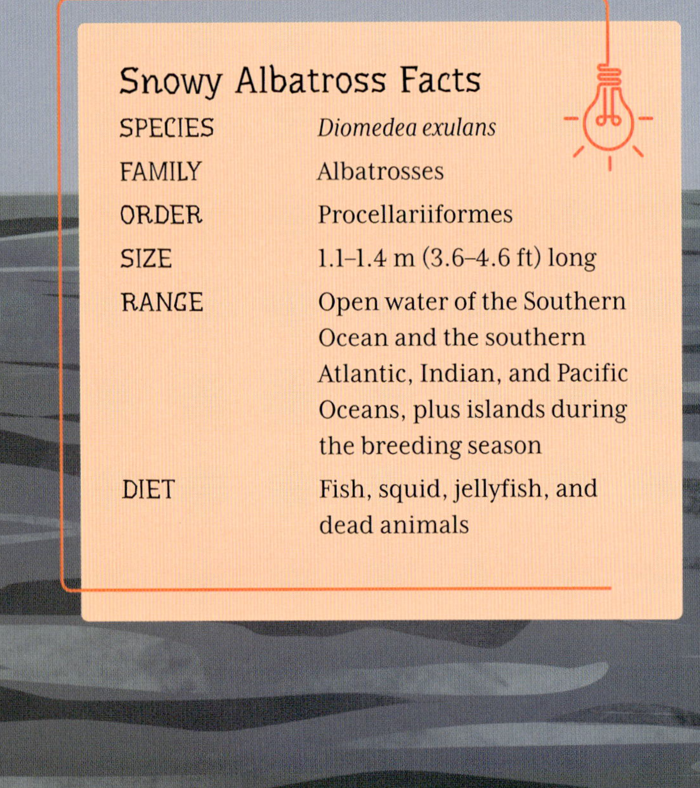

Snowy Albatross Facts

SPECIES	*Diomedea exulans*
FAMILY	Albatrosses
ORDER	Procellariiformes
SIZE	1.1–1.4 m (3.6–4.6 ft) long
RANGE	Open water of the Southern Ocean and the southern Atlantic, Indian, and Pacific Oceans, plus islands during the breeding season
DIET	Fish, squid, jellyfish, and dead animals

FAR FLIER

The snowy albatross's long, narrow wings—not unlike the wings of a passenger plane—allow it to glide without flapping for several hours at a time. By using so little energy, this bird can stay in the air for long periods, even sleeping as it glides. It returns to land only to breed. However, it does land on the water surface to feed.

Usually feeding far from land, this seabird spots food from the air. It watches for large shoals of fish, squid, or jellyfish, and even floating dead mammals, such as whales and seals. It dives to the surface to grasp food in its beak, sometimes making a shallow dive into the water.

HEADING HOME

This albatross mates only every two years, always on the same remote island. It breeds in large colonies, one of the biggest being the 2,000 pairs that nest on the nearly uninhabited Crozet Islands, 2,400 km (1,500 miles) southeast of South Africa. A female lays one egg in January, during the southern summer.

A chick is around 9 months old before it takes to the air. Until that time, its parents take turns bringing food. Due to attacks by birds such as sheathbills and skuas, only one-third of chicks survive this period. However, if a chick does reach adulthood, it can live for 50 years or more, since adults have few predators.

Scientists have studied how albatrosses find their way to the same remote island across a vast ocean, without ever getting lost. They think that the birds navigate by watching the sun and stars, and even by using their sense of smell. In addition, they seem to sense the Earth's magnetic field. The Earth behaves like a giant magnet, with north and south poles, due to the churning iron in its core. Humans can use a magnetic compass to navigate using the magnetic field.

This seabird often follows fishing boats so it can take any unwanted fish that are thrown overboard. Although the snowy albatross is normally alone as it flies, it may gather in large groups around a boat.

In Antarctica

With air temperatures as low as -60 °C (-76 °F), the icy, wind-battered Antarctic continent is home to few species of animals. However, seabirds visit the continent's coasts and close islands, their numbers rising to 100 million during the spring breeding season.

The only vertebrate (backboned) animals to spend time on Antarctica or its close islands are 6 species of seals and around 46 species of seabirds, which all take their food from the surrounding ocean. The only fully land-living, year-round animals on the mainland are a few tiny invertebrates, which mostly live on the warmer coasts. The biggest of them is the flightless Antarctic midge, just 6 mm (0.2 in) long.

Five of the eighteen species of penguins breed on Antarctica or its close islands: Adélies, chinstraps, emperors, gentoos, and macaronis (see page 98). Other Antarctic nesters include albatrosses, gulls, petrels, skuas, and terns.

SOUTH POLAR SKUA

This seabird is one of the few that has been seen—after being blown off course by storms—at the South Pole, which is in the middle of the Antarctic continent. The bird nests on Antarctic coasts in spring, but spends the winter at sea, where it often steals fish from gulls and terns.

GENTOO PENGUIN

This penguin can reach an underwater swimming speed of 36 km/h (22 miles per hour), as it flaps its wings as if "flying" through the water, in pursuit of small fish. Like all penguins, the gentoo cannot fly in air, since its wings are too short and paddle-like.

ADÉLIE PENGUIN

Like all adult penguins, the Adélie has a white underside and black back. When swimming, the penguin's pale belly is difficult to spot from below against the sunlight. From above, its black back is hidden against the darkness. This camouflage helps it catch krill and avoid its main predators: leopard seals.

CHINSTRAP PENGUIN

The chinstrap is kept warm by thick layers of fat and feathers. It spends the winter in the ocean, which has a temperature no lower than -1.8 °C (28.8 °F). In spring, when the air temperature rises, the penguin builds a circular nest from rocks. Both parents take turns warming their two eggs.

SNOW PETREL

The snow petrel has one of the most southerly breeding ranges of any bird, nesting in spring not only on the Antarctic coast but as far as 440 km (270 miles) inland. In winter, it stays at sea, taking frequent rests on the sea ice, where its thick, snow-white feathers are effective camouflage.

EMPEROR PENGUIN

The emperor is the biggest penguin, reaching 1.2 m (3.9 ft) long. It is the only vertebrate that mates on Antarctica in winter, giving it the coldest nesting conditions of any bird. To survive this, it nests in large colonies that cluster together for warmth. Each pair's single egg and chick are warmed on its parents' feet.

Great Frigatebird

Male and female great frigatebirds look quite different from each other. This is known as sexual dimorphism (which means "two forms" in ancient Greek). The female is larger, with wings up to 2.3 m (7.5 ft) wide, and has a white chest. The male has a red throat pouch, which he inflates to attract a female.

FLYING FOR FLYING FISH

Compared with its body weight, this seabird has the largest wings of any bird. The wider-winged snowy albatross has a weight of up to 16.1 kg (35 lb), but the great frigatebird weighs just 1.3 kg (2.9 lb). This makes the great frigatebird an effortless long-distance flier. However, the frigatebird makes very little preen oil, so its feathers are not waterproof and would become heavy if soaked with water. This means that it cannot land on the ocean surface. For this reason, the bird feeds mainly on flying fish, which frequently launch themselves out of the water using their winglike fins.

ATTRACTING A MATE

This frigatebird nests on remote islands, usually in a large colony. At the start of the breeding season, males sit in bushes and trees, then push air into their red throat pouch. They also shake their wings, wag their head, and call. Before choosing a mate, females fly around to watch several males. Once a pair has formed, the male collects twigs and leaves, while the female constructs a nest in a bush or tree.

A male and female great frigatebird form a pair that lasts for one breeding season, but they find a new mate for the next season. Since these birds start to mate at around 10 years old and may live for 40 years, they have many mates during their lives.

A CAREFUL PARENT

Animals have different strategies for making sure that some of their babies survive. Some have lots of babies but give them no care after birth, since a few of the many will probably survive without help. The great frigatebird has an opposite strategy, similar to the one used by humans: It lays a single egg in each breeding season, then takes extreme care. In fact, this bird cares for its chicks for longer than almost any other bird: up to 2 years. As a result, female great frigatebirds breed once every 2 years at the most.

A chick is guarded constantly for the first month of its life, but then it spends periods alone while both parents hunt. Parents feed the chick by regurgitation, spitting up partly digested food that the chick takes from their mouth.

Great Frigatebird Facts

SPECIES	*Fregata minor*
FAMILY	Frigatebirds
ORDER	Suliformes
SIZE	85–105 cm (33–41 in) long
RANGE	Open water of the warm Atlantic, Indian, and Pacific Oceans, plus islands during the breeding season
DIET	Flying fish, plus some other surface fish and squid

Questions and Answers

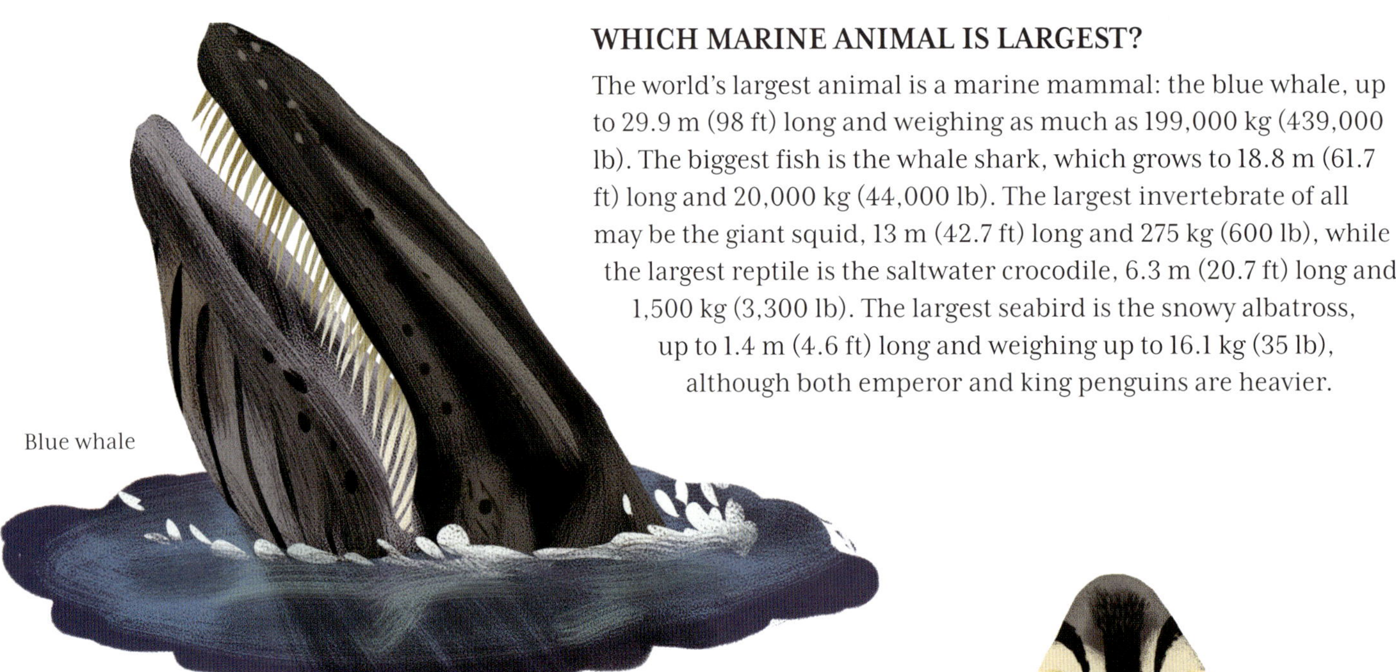

Blue whale

WHICH MARINE ANIMAL IS LARGEST?

The world's largest animal is a marine mammal: the blue whale, up to 29.9 m (98 ft) long and weighing as much as 199,000 kg (439,000 lb). The biggest fish is the whale shark, which grows to 18.8 m (61.7 ft) long and 20,000 kg (44,000 lb). The largest invertebrate of all may be the giant squid, 13 m (42.7 ft) long and 275 kg (600 lb), while the largest reptile is the saltwater crocodile, 6.3 m (20.7 ft) long and 1,500 kg (3,300 lb). The largest seabird is the snowy albatross, up to 1.4 m (4.6 ft) long and weighing up to 16.1 kg (35 lb), although both emperor and king penguins are heavier.

WHICH BIRD CAN SPEND LONGEST UNDERWATER?

The emperor penguin can dive for the longest time: up to 27 minutes. It has been seen as far as 535 m (1,755 ft) below the surface. To survive so long without taking a breath of air, it slows its heart to 15 beats per minute and shuts down its non-essential organs.

WHICH ANIMAL SWIMS FASTEST?

The fastest swimmer may be the Indo-Pacific sailfish, which has been recorded moving at 54 km/h (34 miles per hour) and may even reach 110 km/h (68 miles per hour) over short distances. The fish's muscular, streamlined body grows to 3 m (9.8 ft) long. It raises its sail-like dorsal fin only when attacking smaller fish, to steady itself against sideways movements.

WHICH ANIMAL HAS THE BIGGEST EYES?

The giant squid probably has the largest eyes of any animal: 27 cm (10.6 in) across. These immense eyes help the squid to see in the dark waters up to 300 m (980 ft) below the surface.

WHICH ANIMAL LAYS THE MOST EGGS?

The ocean sunfish lays the most eggs of any animal: up to 300 million in one season. The fish—which has an unusual body shape due to its lack of a tail fin—is also one of the heaviest bony-skeletoned fish, weighing up to 2,300 kg (5,100 lb).

WHICH MARINE ANIMAL LIVES THE LONGEST?

Bowhead whales may be the longest-living mammals of all, reaching more than 200 years old. The bowhead lives longer than any marine reptile or bird, but it does not live as long as the longest-living fish, the Greenland shark, which can live to at least 390 years old. Invertebrates take the record for the longest lives: The immortal jellyfish may live forever, as it can turn itself back into its young form, a polyp, if it is injured or old.

WHICH ANIMAL HAS THE STRONGEST BITE?

The saltwater crocodile may have the most powerful bite of any animal: 16,414 Newtons. A Newton is the force needed to move a stationary weight of 1 kg (2.2 lb) a distance of 1 m (3.3 ft) in 1 second.

Glossary

abdomen
In invertebrates, the abdomen is the back part of the body.

algae
Plantlike living things that usually live in and around water, such as seaweeds.

amphibian
An animal that usually spends part of its life on land and part in fresh water, such as a frog.

anal fin
A fin on a fish's underside, toward the tail.

antenna (plural: antennae)
A slender "feeler" found on the head of some invertebrates.

aposematism
The use of bright markings to warn predators that an animal is not good to eat, usually due to tasting bad or being poisonous.

appendage
A body part (such as a leg) that extends from the body or head.

arthropod
An invertebrate, such as a crab or insect, with a hard covering, or exoskeleton, and jointed legs.

bacterium (plural: bacteria)
A tiny living thing with one cell.

barbel
A whisker-like feeler extending from around the mouth or snout.

bask
To warm up by resting in sunshine.

bay
A coastal area of water that is partly surrounded by land.

bioluminescent
Able to make its own light.

bird
An animal with a toothless beak, wings, and feathers.

bivalve
A soft-bodied invertebrate that lives in a hinged, two-part shell.

breeding season
The time of year when animals are mating.

camouflage
The way the pattern and shape of an animal make it less visible in its habitat.

carapace
The hard shell covering the back of a turtle or crab.

cartilage
A strong, bendy, lightweight material found in the body.

cell
The smallest working part of a living thing's body.

cephalopod
A mollusk, such as an octopus, with a large head and arms or tentacles.

cephalothorax
In some arthropods, the cephalothorax is a joined head and thorax.

cetacean
A water-living mammal with a streamlined body and two flippers; a whale, dolphin, or porpoise.

class
A scientific group that includes animals with the same body plan, such as birds or mammals.

cnidarian
A water-living animal with stinging cells, such as a jellyfish, coral, or sea anemone.

colony
A group of animals living together.

coral reef
An underwater structure made of the skeletons of millions of tiny animals called coral polyps.

crustacean
An arthropod, such as a crab, with two pairs of antennae on its head.

current
A stream of water that flows through the ocean.

dorsal fin
A fin on the back of a fish or cetacean.

echolocation
Making calls and listening to the echoes of those calls, in order to find the way and locate prey.

evolve
To change gradually over time.

exoskeleton
The hard covering of some invertebrates.

extinction
When a species dies out completely.

eyespot
An eye-like marking.

family
A group of species that are closely related, so that they look and behave much alike. For example, common and striped dolphins are in the oceanic dolphin family.

fertilize
To make an egg start to develop into a new young animal, by joining it with a male cell.

filter-feed
To strain small animals and other food from water, using comb-like or sieve-like body parts.

fin
A body part that juts from the body of fish and some other water-living animals, helping them swim.

fish
A water-living animal, usually with fins, that takes oxygen from the water using gills.

fresh water
Unsalted water, such as rivers, lakes, and ponds.

gill
An organ that takes oxygen from water.

gland
A body part that makes a substance for use in the body or for release.

global warming
Rising world temperatures caused mainly by human activities.

habitat
The natural home of an animal, plant, or other living thing.

hydrothermal vent
An opening in the seafloor out of which flows hot, mineral-rich water.

inlet
A long, narrow dip in the coastline, where the ocean forms an armlike shape.

intertidal zone
The area on the shore that is below water during high tides and above water when the sea draws out.

invertebrate
An animal without a backbone, such as a squid, crab, or coral.

krill
A small, shrimplike crustacean.

larva (plural: larvae)
A young stage in the life cycle of some invertebrates, fish, and amphibians, during which the animal looks different from its adult form.

lens
A structure at the front of the eye that focusses light.

lung
An organ that takes oxygen from air.

mammal
An animal, such as a whale or human, that grows hair at some point in its life and feeds its young on milk.

mangrove
A tree or shrub that usually lives in the intertidal zone.

marine
Found in the ocean.

marsh
An area of land, either wholly or partly covered by water, where most plants are low grasses, rushes, or reeds.

mate
A partner for reproducing (making new young animals).

maxilliped
In a crustacean, a leglike appendage used for feeding.

metamorphosis
The change in body shape that most amphibians and some invertebrates and fish go through as they grow into adults.

migrate
To move from one region to another at particular times of year.

mineral
A solid that forms in the ground or in water.

mollusk
An invertebrate with a soft body and sometimes a hard shell, such as a snail, slug, or octopus.

mucus
A slimy substance made by some animals.

mudflat
Muddy land that is uncovered when the sea draws out at low tide.

nocturnal
Active at night.

nutrient
A substance needed by an animal's body for growth and health.

order
A group of families that are closely related. For example, the true seal and dog families are in the meat-eating Carnivora order.

organ
A body part that does a particular job, such as the heart or brain.

oxygen
A gas found in air and water that is needed by animals' cells for releasing energy from food.

parasite
A living thing that lives in, on, or around another living thing, taking food and other benefits from it.

pectoral fin
One of a pair of fins on either side of a fish, just behind its head.

pelvic fin
One of a pair of fins on the underside of a fish.

phylum
A scientific group that includes closely related classes. For example, the phylum of arthropods includes classes such as insects and sea spiders.

plant
A living thing that makes its own food from sunlight.

planula
The swimming larva of a cnidarian such as a coral.

pleopod
In a crustacean, a leglike appendage used for swimming.

plumage
A bird's covering of feathers.

plunge-diving
A hunting style used by some seabirds, when they drop from a height into water to catch prey.

polar
In the areas close to the poles, where it is very cold all year.

polyp
The sessile, or non-moving, life stage of invertebrates such as corals.

predator
An animal that hunts other animals.

preen gland
An organ at the base of a bird's tail, which produces oil used for keeping feathers healthy and waterproof.

prey
An animal that is killed by another animal for food.

range
The area where an animal is found.

reptile
An animal with a dry skin, covered in scales, that usually lays eggs on land.

roost
To rest or sleep.

salt water
Water, such as ocean water, that contains minerals including salt.

scale
A small, hard plate that protects the skin of most fish and reptiles.

schooling
When a group of fish are swimming in the same direction.

scute
A thick, bony plate found in some reptiles.

sea ice
Ice that forms on the surface of the ocean in polar regions.

segment
A section or part.

sessile
Fixed in one place.

shoal
A group of fish.

siphon
A tube used for liquid.

snout
The nose and mouth of an animal.

species
A group of living things that look similar and can mate together.

sperm
A cell made by a male animal, which joins with a female's egg cell to make a new living thing.

streamlined
Smoothly shaped, making it possible to travel easily through water.

suction
Removing liquid or air from a space so that something else is sucked in to fill the gap.

symbiosis
When two species live closely together.

temperate
In the areas between the tropics and polar regions, where it is neither very hot nor very cold.

tentacle
A long, thin body part, used for feeling or grabbing.

thorax
In an invertebrate, the part of the body between the head and abdomen.

tide
The rising and falling of the ocean at the shore, caused by the pull of the Moon's gravity on the water.

tropical
In the area around the equator, where it is very hot all year.

ultraviolet
A form of sunlight that cannot be seen by humans.

venom
A deadly or dangerous chemical made by an animal.

vertebrate
An animal with a backbone: a fish, amphibian, reptile, bird, or mammal.

webbed feet
Having toes that are linked by tissue and skin, making them paddle-like.

wingspan
The distance across a bird's wings, from wingtip to wingtip.

zooplankton
Tiny animals, larvae, and eggs that drift through the ocean.

Index